ON THE ROAD AGAIN

Printed in the United States of America

89 90 91 92 93 5 4 3 2 1

Library of Congress Cataloging-in-Publication Data

Davis, Jason, 1939–
    On the road again.

    1. Davis, Jason, 1939–   . 2. Television journalists—Minnesota—
Biography.   3. Television producers and directors—Minnesota—
Biography.   4. On the road again (Television program)   5. Television feature
stories.
I. Title.
PN4874.D373A3   1989   791.45'0232'092 [B]   89-22483
ISBN 0-89658-108-X

Published by Voyageur Press, Inc.
P.O. Box 338
123 North Second Street
Stillwater, MN 55082 U.S.A.
In Minn. 612-430-2210
Toll Free 800-888-9653

Voyageur Press books are also available at discounts in bulk quantities for premium or sales-promotion use. For details contact the Marketing Manager. Please write or call for our free catalog of publications.

ON THE ROAD AGAIN

BY
JASON DAVIS

Jason.

VOYAGEUR PRESS

Some day each of us will be famous for fifteen minutes.

—*Andy Warhol*

ACKNOWLEDGMENTS

I STARTED TRAVELING when I was fifteen years old, first as a merchant seaman sailing out of the Port of London for nearly ten years, then as a salesman selling, of all things, cash registers for a Norwegian company in Britain and Australia. For the past twenty-one years, I have traveled as a reporter in Australia and the United States. Along the way, I have been helped and encouraged by many people, and they all must take some credit for this book.

More specifically, I wish to thank the people who populate these pages and those hundreds we have visited whose stories we've told on television over the years. I never cease to be amazed at the trust and friendliness we receive every week as we go about our strange business. How easily people accept a bunch of complete strangers into their homes and often their lives. How freely they speak to us and share their interests. How unaware they seem of the unblinking eye of the camera that is our tool for gathering their story.

At least half the credit, often much more, must go to the long-suffering but highly talented photographers, who not only shoot the film or tape for "On the Road Again" but spend many hours editing the material before it gets on the air. I have taken care to include their names in the stories, so I don't need to list them here, but I do always number them among my friends.

The single person most responsible for any success I may have had producing feature stories for KSTP-TV is the owner of the station. Stanley S. Hubbard is a man who has never stood in my way if I assured him the project was worthy of the cost. He is a man with a sense of adventure who isn't afraid to "put his money where his mouth is."

And I owe everything to my wife, Amanda, and my children, Kylie, Verity, Jessica, and Jeremy, who maintain a happy, healthy, and loving home during my absences and even manage to keep it all going when I am home.

CONTENTS

Hiccup Charlie   *1*
A Mixed-Up Whooping Crane Named Tex   *7*
Grant County's Most Famous Citizen   *13*
Papa Gringo   *19*
King of the Worms   *25*
Power at Last   *29*
Alvera   *33*
Peter in a Pith Helmet   *39*
Save the Whales   *43*
Stanley's Store   *63*
Miracle of Moorhead   *69*
Last Needle   *73*
Roye Rodgers   *77*
The Reluctant Lady of McGarvey Shoal   *81*
Kids Who Eat Flowers   *95*
A Doctor for El Casco   *101*
A Dog You Can Count On   *109*
North to the Pole   *113*
The Dog Lady of Esko   *127*
Raccoons Make Lousy Pets   *131*
The Wilderness Family   *135*
A Friend in Time   *145*
Minnesota by Thanksgiving   *149*
Rainbow Love   *175*
Pesky Pants for Christmas   *179*

HICCUP CHARLIE

WHEN WE DECIDED to make a regular segment of the features I had been producing at KSTP-TV for a year or two, we began to look around for stories that were, in the first place, *unique*. We cast our net wide: Minnesota, Wisconsin, both the Dakotas, and, to our south, Iowa. Our colleagues, families, and friends were all enthusiastic, and the ideas just poured in. Unfortunately, most suggestions were not at all suitable for a television feature story, but now and again, we found a pearl.

Charlie Osborne was a pearl. A feature producer's dream, and, to clinch the matter, he lived in our patch. Charlie's hometown was Anthon, Iowa, and Charlie had the hiccups. Not just the bothersome bouts we all get from time to time after eating or drinking too much or too fast. No, Charlie, who was eighty-six years old, had had the hiccups for *fifty-six years.*

Cameraman Bill Juntunen and I found ourselves outside Charlie's house one spring day in 1978. It was a small frame home on a residential street in the quiet backwater town that is Anthon, Iowa. Charlie opened the door. He was alone now since his wife had died the year before.

The front door opened into the main sitting room of the house, and it was apparent that Charlie spent most of his time there. A rumpled blanket on a couch at the side of the room showed where he slept. There was a lot of furniture in the room, older stuff mostly, overstuffed chairs, and a hat stand carrying more than its share of coats and hats. Beside the old rocker Charlie sank into after letting us in was a large brass spittoon, and it wasn't being used as a planter either.

Charlie looked old. He had no teeth, and he needed a shave. He wore a pair of baggy pants topped by a blue flannel shirt and a button-up sweater.

It wasn't immediately apparent that we were in the presence of the world's champion hiccuper. I mean, he wasn't making any unusual noise or jerking around in any way. But he assured us he was hiccuping regularly between twenty and forty times a minute. I had to be sure that the viewers of our program would have no doubt about Charlie's claim, so I asked him just to sit still, face the camera, and relax. Sure enough, as he sat there staring impassively at the lens, Charlie was hiccuping gently every few seconds. It was a strange sight, the old man sitting there just hiccuping.

It was time for the interview, and Charlie seemed resigned to the ritual as we fussed around with lights and hung a small microphone on the neck of his sweater. After all, he told us, he had been a kind of celebrity for most of his life, ever since that day more than half a century before when he had been preparing to butcher a large pig. Charlie wanted to hang that big porker from a tree to make it easier to cut up, so he grabbed it around the middle, grunted, and lifted. He got the pig hung nicely but immediately began hiccuping. And he hadn't stopped since!

2

The 1989 edition of the *Guinness Book of World Records* carries essentially the same information it has for years on who holds the record for "Hiccoughing."

> The longest recorded attack of hiccoughs is that which afflicted Charles Osborne (b. Dec. 18 1894) of Anthon, Iowa, from 1922 for 66 years. He contracted it when slaughtering a hog and hiccoughed about 430 million times in the interim period. He was unable to find a cure, but led a reasonably normal life in which he had two wives and fathered eight children. He did admit, however, that he could not keep in his false teeth. In July 1986, his rate went up to 20–25 times from 10 hics per minute in 1985, and an earlier high of 40.*

Well, we are now ahead of ourselves. It is still only 1978, and Charlie is steaming along at about 30 hiccups, or hiccoughs, a minute. And Charlie hasn't given up hope of a cure. "Maybe there is a way I can get rid of 'em," says Charlie forlornly. If there is, perhaps it's in the hundreds of letters Charlie gets from all over the world every week. It seems just about everyone on earth has heard of Charlie's predicament, which is not surprising when you learn that back in the 1930s, Charlie was invited to New York to appear on the popular radio show "Ripley's Believe It or Not."

In fact, Charlie told us that that particular appearance was less than successful. "They paid for me to go to New York, put me up in a fancy hotel for eight days, and gave me fifty dollars a day spending money." Charlie's eyes shone with the memory of such an adventure. "Trouble was, I was so excited by the whole thing, when the time came for me to go on the radio, I didn't have the hiccups!"

* From the *Guinness Book of World Records*, published by Sterling Publishing Co., Inc., New York, N.Y. Copyright 1989 by Guinness Publishing Ltd.

But back to Charlie's voluminous mail. As we sat facing each other in his room in Anthon, Charlie tipped his head at a large cardboard box sitting on the floor literally overflowing with letters. Most of them were unopened. "That's just what's come in this week," said Charlie morosely. "I can't read 'em, so it's a waste of time."

Charlie was illiterate. There was no way he could read the hundreds of cards and letters written in English let alone the contents of dozens of envelopes with exotic stamps that had come from the four corners of the world. With his permission, I opened some of the envelopes. By and large, they contained those well-known "cures" for hiccups such as Stand on your head and drink a glass of water, Drop a cold key down your neck, and Hold your breath for three minutes.

We discovered that Charlie had a great sense of humor when he began to tell us of some of the more unusual cures he had heard of and even tried. "One lady told me to scrape a pertater. Lay on my back and scrape a pertater real fine and lay it on my navel." Charlie gave us a toothless smile and continued. "And all such things as that. And drink water out of a glass upside down, and sugar and vinegar. Oh, my God, it's awful."

Charlie had piqued my interest. "Did you try shaving 'pertater' into your navel? I asked, trying to mimic him so he wouldn't think I was a snob. "Yes, I tried that," Charlie said firmly. "Did you think that might work?" I asked. "I thought it might work." Charlie was a man of few words. "I scraped this pertater real fine like she said to do it. I laid on my back down on that couch over there and laid it on my navel for thirty minutes." I couldn't help but say, "Didn't you feel foolish?" Charlie snorted, "Yeah, I felt foolish."

Needless to say, it didn't work. Charlie said the only thing that seemed to have any effect on his pesky hiccups was dam-

4

son preserves. He said one mouthful would stop the breathing spasms for hours.

One popular cure that Charlie said definitely doesn't work is sudden shock. "Now, I've had people try and scare me. One guy stepped up behind me with a double-barreled shotgun and let it off." Charlie shook his head with resignation. "It had no effect."

We left Charlie sitting in his lonely room in Anthon, Iowa, with only the regular sounds of his own hiccups to keep him company. We didn't expect to see him again, but we were wrong.

In 1986, I was shooting some stories in the region around Brainerd, Minnesota. After producing "On the Road Again" for ten years, it had become a well-known segment anywhere KSTP-TV could be seen. People often came up to us on the street or in restaurants to introduce themselves or, more often than not, to suggest a story to us. And this day in Brainerd, someone had an idea. "Have you seen the story in the Brainerd paper about the guy with hiccups?" Well, I knew that stories about poor old Charlie often surfaced, but as far as I knew, he was still living in Anthon, Iowa.

Surprise. Charlie was now living with his daughter near Brainerd, and he still had the hiccups.

Charlie's daughter Lucretia lived in Aitkin, Minnesota, and because her father was ninety-four now and ailing, she had persuaded him to stay with her and her husband in their attractive lakeside home. Charlie looked thinner and more worn than he had eight years before. Someone had updated his hiccup count to 450 million, and he looked as if he remembered every one. Sure enough, there was the ever-present box of mail, and Charlie was just as skeptical as ever. "I've tried a lot of ideas but don't do any good."

It occurred to me that there must be a silver lining to this tale of nearly sixty-five years of misery. "If you hadn't had the hiccups all these years, you would have missed a lot of things, wouldn't you?" I asked, trying to be bright and cheerful. "You've met a lot of people, traveled to different places, made many new friends." "Yeah," Charlie said, without conviction. Undeterred, I plowed on, frantically trying to find something positive that he could agree with. "People write to you from all over the world. Don't you think, in some ways, having the hiccups wasn't so bad?" I was getting somewhere. Charlie was smiling. My next sentence let Charlie in. "After all, your life would have been pretty dull without them." "I would have rather lived a quiet life without 'em!" said Charlie emphatically.

Maybe, somewhere, there is a cure for Charlie Osborne's hiccups. Charlie is old and tired. And his daughter Lucretia knows what he would like more than anything else in the world. "I just would like to see my Dad without them just for a week before he dies."

A MIXED-UP
WHOOPING CRANE
NAMED TEX

WE HADN'T BEEN working long together, Bill Juntunen and I, and "On the Road Again" was only a few months old, so when he said his wife, Michelle, had an idea for a story for us, I was a little doubtful.

When I heard the idea, I was astounded. Michelle claimed she had heard of a man in Wisconsin somewhere who danced with a crane. A crane! I tried my utmost to visualize a human being cavorting with a metallic monster, but it was too incongruous even for me. "No," said Bill, "not a crane . . . a crane, a bird with a long neck and legs like chopsticks."

The International Crane Foundation is in Baraboo, Wisconsin. Its director is George Archibald, and I liked him the minute I set eyes on him. George happily admitted that he did indeed dance with a crane, an incredibly mixed-up whooping crane named Tex. Tex, a female bird, had been raised by hand and had "imprinted" on her handlers. Tex thought she was human. This wouldn't normally be a problem, but Tex was one of fewer than a hundred of these rare birds left in the world. Whooping cranes are a very endangered species. Apart from a damaged wing, Tex was a perfectly normal female bird. The International Crane Foundation is dedicated to saving these magnificent animals, but how can you breed a bird that doesn't think she's a bird and thinks any mate she would have should look like a human being—a human being like George Archibald?

"They are monogamous birds, and I'm her mate, so to speak." George beamed as he confirmed that he had to be the stimulus that would bring Tex into breeding condition so she could be artificially inseminated with the hope that a fertile egg would result. So every spring, George would spend an hour or two each day in Tex's pen *dancing*. That's, apparently, how cranes do it. The courtship ritual centers on a complex dance routine that is an essential preamble to a successful mating.

So the stage was set. George ambled into Tex's pen while Bill rolled the camera. And they danced and danced, pranced and cavorted, the man and the white bird with the red feathers in her head. George flapped his arms wildly and jumped in the air, and the bird did the same, but with a lot more elegance. They whirled around each other, Tex arching her neck with passion only another crane could understand or respond to. George began to pant . . . with exhaustion. "Have you got enough film, Bill?" George gasped between sets. Bill was mesmerized by the sight of a man dancing with a big bird and was slow to respond. "Yeah, for now," he finally admitted as he tore his right eye away from a camera eyepiece that had revealed such wonders.

I was delighted. I knew instinctively we had just recorded a remarkable sequence, and I was in a hurry to get the film back to the Twin Cities, get it processed, and get it on the air. As we packed our equipment into the car, I asked George how long he could continue this grueling regimen. "Well, to tell you the truth, Jason, I can't keep it up much longer. So far, Tex has failed to produce a fertile egg after several years of this. But we can't quit as long as she is healthy. I have too many demands on my time, though, to spend each spring dancing with a bird."

The next conversation I had with George would lead us halfway around the world and into the next episode of the remarkable story of a thoroughly mixed-up whooping crane named Tex.

But first we had a television feature to produce. We arrived back in the Twin Cities too late to begin working on the story that day, but it was spinning in my head as I drove home. It was in the shower that I knew what would enhance an already wonderful story. What is dancing without music? The "Blue Danube" waltz, that's it. I could hardly wait to tell Bill, so I called him at his home. "Bill, try running the 'Blue Danube' behind the sequence of George dancing with Tex when you start editing tomorrow." It worked beyond my wildest dreams. It was perfect, and it wasn't only Bill and I who thought so. That very night, the story of the man who danced with a whooping crane was shown on ABC's "World News Tonight" and subsequently transmitted by satellite around the world.

We hadn't heard the last of Tex and George Archibald by any means. George, as you may remember, had told us he was too busy to continue spending his summers dancing with Tex. He had also told us there was someone in this wide world of ours who would.

A few months later, we had our camera set up on the busiest street in the world. The Ginza in Tokyo, Japan, is a major downtown shopping and business center, and among the thousands of people on their way to work there that day was a young man with a mission. As the camera picked him out

9

of the crowd, my narration would explain that this was twenty-two-year-old Yoshimitsu Shigata, a Japanese ornithologist who had volunteered, despite having been married for just six short months, to go to Baraboo, Wisconsin, U.S.A. There, in that far-off place, he would spend the upcoming summer trying to convince a particularly mixed-up whooping crane named Tex that he was a suitable mate. Yoshi, like George, belonged to a unique group numbering, as far as I knew, just two. Yoshi was a genuine bird lover.

George had come to Japan for several reasons, but the one we were interested in was his handing over to Yoshi the secrets to Tex's heart. We arranged to meet George and Yoshi at Ueno Zoo in the heart of Tokyo. The two men were sitting on a bench beside a pool of water and a cage containing some sandhill cranes. George was patiently trying to explain to Yoshi, who spoke very little English, the finer points of crane foreplay. "When she doesn't want to be with you or close to you, she starts to preen her shoulders, fix her feathers. The red is very large on her head, and this means in visual language 'I don't want to dance anymore.' "

George had a large notebook on his lap full of sketches and diagrams. Yoshi couldn't read the English notes, but he nodded his head enthusiastically as George continued. "Now, this is called the unison call. It's a duet between the male and the female crane. So Tex will want to unison call with you quite a bit and," said George pointing at the pencil drawings in the book, "this is a territorial threat but it's also a sexual display." Until this point in the impromptu lesson in bird biology, the passing crowds had paid little attention to the good-looking, young, smiling caucasian and his young, attentive Japanese friend. But startled glances and grins of amusement flowed like ripples on a pond when George launched into his version of the mating call of a whooping crane. "*Whoop, whop, whoop.*

You go *whoop, whop, whoop.*" Dutifully, but with less volume, Yoshi echoed, "*Whoop, whop, whoop.*" He was on his way.

A few weeks later, we were all back at the International Crane Foundation in Baraboo, Wisconsin. It was Yoshi's first day on the job, and we were there to record his introduction to Tex. I don't know what Tex thought, but I was surprised to see how far this young ornithologist was prepared to go to win the bird's heart. Yoshi was dressed in snow-white coveralls, and on his head perched a little red beanie. He looked uncertain as the door to Tex's pen swung open. At first, nothing happened. We all stood there waiting and watching the black opening behind the pen door. Then, suddenly, the tall, spindly, white bird strutted out, took one look at poor Yoshi in his white suit and red hat, and strode away never to look back.

Yoshi went back to Japan and to his wife. Presumably, they lived happily ever after. As for Tex, it was obviously George or nothing.

The following summer, George lived in a ramshackle hut in a field at the International Crane Foundation. His only company was a lovesick whooping crane named Tex. And after several efforts at artificial insemination, Tex did lay a fertile egg. It was carefully incubated in a machine and watched over day and night by skilled technicians, and one day it hatched. George immediately dubbed the chick the only name that seemed appropriate after so much trouble. He named the chick "Gee Whiz."

GRANT COUNTY'S
MOST FAMOUS
CITIZEN

THE HAND-PAINTED sign nailed to the tree at the intersection of two rural highways in Grant County, Minnesota, read:

We knew we were in the right place. Ever since he'd had a small write-up in the local paper, Harvey Reynolds had reveled in his notoriety. He didn't know we were coming to ask him to allow us to produce a television feature story about his new-found fame, but we were sure he wouldn't mind.

The driveway was long, winding, unkept, and it seemed to go on forever. It didn't help that we had no idea what to expect. I had just read a small article in an out-of-town newspaper that told of a local character who spent his life fixing machines. Two-cycle machines, that is. Lawn mowers and tillers, things like that.

Our first thought was that we had taken a wrong turn somewhere and driven into the town dump. Lying around a group of ramshackle buildings was a small mountain range of junk. It wound like a ribbon around the sheds and dilapidated house and peaked where several old appliances were stacked in a teetering pile. The valleys were strewn with boulderlike parts of ancient and long-dead machines. We would have turned around and gone back but for the sound of something banging in the black depths of a shed that looked as if it had just barely survived an earthquake.

Cameraman Ian Logan and I hadn't come this far because of our lack of curiosity. "Hello, anyone there?" I called. The banging abruptly stopped, and a second later Harvey Reynolds appeared. It was his glasses that you noticed first. They were heavy, black, horn-rimmed, and they had seen better days. Both sides of the frames were taped together with a heavy layer of black electrician's tape, and from behind the glass shone two bright, anxious-to-please eyes. His balding pate was surrounded by a shock of hair that hadn't seen a comb or a brush for quite a while, and his unshaven face carried an extra load of grime from the engine he had been working on before we arrived.

His face split into a grin, exposing a set of teeth that resem-

14

bled my childhood memories of rows of bombed houses. "How you doin'?" were the first words out of his mouth. They were not the last. For the next two hours, Harvey never stopped. The man's enthusiasm for his junk and life never waned. Beneath the dirty blue shirt and bright red suspenders beat the heart of a true fanatic.

"I know you've come to see my bikes. Come on over here and I'll show. Just stand there a minute while I get this door open and I'll show you sumpin you never seen in your whole life. I'll betcha you never seen anything like this. I made 'em all myself, and there ain't any like it anywhere."

The man never stopped to take a breath. As he talked incessantly, he struggled to extricate a tangled mass of bright orange steel tubing and wire spoke wheels that turned out to be one of his "famous" bikes. Harvey, you see, spent a lot of his time, I won't call it spare time because it appeared all of his time was spare, making bikes. They were made from the legion of parts he scavenged on his weekly forays to the local dumps and the backs of factories and warehouses in the region. He made bicycles, tricycles, and quadricycles. They were uniformly bright orange—for no reason, except that somewhere, sometime, Harvey had picked up a lot of free orange paint.

Sixty-year-old Harvey Reynolds, son of a farmer who broke his heart trying to turn this marginal land into a crop-producing living, had never left home, never traveled farther than sixty miles from his driveway, and, in response to my question, never married. "Why not?" I asked. "I dunno. Like it like it is. Come and go as you want. Go fishin' a lot. Fix a bike and go and pick up cans. Good excercise." As he spoke, Harvey reached down into a pile of nearby junk and picked out a rusty piece of ducting with a fan-drive wheel protruding from one side. He spun the wheel and said with such pride you had to admire it, "See how it turns?"

15

We had only been listening to Harvey for about ten minutes when it became apparent that alone with only his junk for company, he had evolved his own language. One dubious looking contraption he said was his "snow-bile." (Worked, too, he said.) Another Rube Goldberg lookalike was his "self-compelled mower," and he had stacks of very valuable "luminum." Never watched "terberision" but amused himself by making all kinds of gadgets like his "lecit circuit saw." We had to weave through the major part of his outdoor warehouse to see his homemade "lecit *chain* saw." The chain saw actually worked, but with a motor hanging off the handle that must have weighed thirty pounds, it wasn't very practical. But the best was yet to come.

"Now I'll show you sumpin. One pull on this rope and this motor goin' to be runnin'." The motor was a fifty-year-old single-cylinder Wisconsin sticking out of the front of a large contraption that defied our efforts at definition. I walked back about twenty feet to try and get the whole machine in perspective in the vain hope it would give itself away. No good. I sidled up to Ian, who was busy trying to keep the scampering little man with the grimy hands and broken nails in his viewfinder. "What the hell is it, Ian?" I whispered. He just shrugged. I wasn't going to get any help there.

In the meantime, Harvey was winding an oily piece of rope around a mangled pulley that was on the front of the engine. "I'll show you guys. One pull on this rope and this motor gonna start straight off. You believe it? You just watch this. Never had anything that will operate on one pull very often." I looked at Ian to make sure he was ready to record this historic event and nodded to Harvey. With all the confidence he could muster in his slight frame, Harvey jerked on the rope. The engine spun over and croaked. "Damn near went, didn't it?" said Harvey. "Nearly went, nearly went," I said back as encouragingly as I could. To give him his due, Harvey did

16

start the engine on the second try, and with a rapid series of pulls and twists on the dozens of levers that stuck at all angles out of the body of the thing, it lurched into motion.

It was only when Harvey, standing regally at the rear of the lumbering mixture of junk with an engine out front, steered it into a nearby field that we realized what he was driving was the tractor he had told us earlier he had "remodeled." I don't remember ever seeing a happier man. Harvey just beamed as he chugged back to us and yelled, "Yeah, that was a good one, wasn't it?"

There is a postscript to our tale of Harvey Reynolds and his uniqueness. I had a call a couple of months after we had visited him from someone who said he was a friend. Did we know that Harvey's house had burned down? No, we did not. Did we know that Harvey was so loved by the people in the surrounding community that they had located a trailer house and had set it up for him? No, we did not, but the next time we were in the area, we would be happy to swing by and see how he was getting on.

It looked pretty much the same to us when we got back to Harvey's piece of Minnesota. The acreage was still producing little more than a thin crop of rust on the piles of old machinery and junk. Certainly, the old house was gone, but we had hardly noticed it among the other ruins when we were last there anyway. In its place stood a twenty-foot plywood trailer, and from it sprang the same old Harvey Reynolds. The first thing we noticed was that he was wearing ill-fitting but new-looking clothes. Even new glasses. From the trailer, the faint sounds of country western music trickled out as Harvey welcomed us by launching into a vivid description of the conflagration that had taken away his home. "Fire everywhere," he said. "Happened so quick couldn't save much." "What did you manage to save, Harvey?" I asked. "Jest a minute." Back he went into the trailer to reappear a few seconds

17

later clutching about eight old long-playing records, still in their sleeves, that were charred all around the edges. "Is this what you saved, Harvey?" "Yeah, my Patsy Cline music. She's the best, you know. I'll tell you, that Patsy." It was obvious these old records had come close to meltdown during the fire. If that was the case, Harvey must have risked his life to save them. "Well, I only had to go about six feet, so I just feel my way and back out again that quick . . . 'cos I knew where they was." I was surprised to discover Harvey was a music lover.

The records were the only thing Harvey had left, but he seemed completely happy and undeterred, because Harvey, the loner, had neighbors who cared about him. "I think I got nice friends. I've known that for a long time," he said. "Does that make you feel good, Harvey?" I asked. "Real good. To have friends like that, when you need them most, they're there."

PAPA GRINGO

He STRODE CONFIDENTLY across the large open square in the center of one of the world's most dangerous cities, a deeply tanned man wearing dark blue pants, a blue shirt, and denim jacket. The sleeves of both the shirt and the jacket were turned back in casual recognition of the temperate climate of Bogota, Colombia.

Ward Bentley was well into his fifties, but it was only the surprising splash of grey in his generous eyebrows that gave him away. Otherwise, this athletic-looking man with the mop of dark hair looked like a young tourist out for a walk, with perhaps his lunch and a guidebook in the brown canvas bag that hung from his shoulder and swung by his side.

Cameraman Russ Brown and I had come to this South American city for several reasons. We were tracking donated medical supplies from hospitals in Minnesota to destitute clinics in the interior of this country, which was ravaged by drug cartels and much fighting between illegal white settlers

19

and the indigenous Indians. And we were interested in a program of the Shriners Hospital for Crippled Children in Minneapolis that was making six beds available for kids from Colombia who had no hope of similar care in their own country.

Colombia, particularly its capital city, Bogota, was, and indeed still is, a hazardous place to be. So who was this gringo who walked with so little concern in this place that the travel agents warn against visiting let alone wandering around in?

"I had half a century of making a lot of money like we are told we are supposed to do, so I decided for my second half century I'd do something more important," he told us as we three stood collecting a curious crowd on a corner of one of the many squares that make this such an attractive city. We had been told by many people that Ward was an unusual man and well worth tracking down where he worked, the streets of Bogota.

Giving up "the good life" as a photographer in the United States, he had made a conscious decision to devote the rest of his life to easing the suffering of a forgotten people. Not some remote tribe of Indians living in the jungle or an exotic race on a tropical island in the South Pacific, nothing as glamorous as that. Ward had dedicated himself to the street children of the world, and what better place to start than Bogota, Colombia?

When we were there, Bogota had at least five thousand children who lived by their wits on its crowded, filthy, crime-ridden streets. There is even a special word in Spanish for them. They are called *gamines*. As a group, they are amazingly young. We saw little girls and boys who couldn't have been older than four years reaching up above their heads to wipe the windows of cars trapped at stoplights for a peso or two. One little girl vigorously scrubbed a side window that was halfway down on the driver's side of a big, shiny car. The woman driver could only see the grimy little face, but we could see the threadbare red sweater covering a too-short dirty white dress revealing grubby, ill-fitting underpants. The driver passed a coin out of the window into a tiny little hand. It would buy bread, perhaps, or maybe be passed along to the older kids for drugs. No one really knew, or cared. The children are homeless, scratching a living somehow by any means possible, legal or, more likely, illegal. Fifteen-year-old prostitutes melted into dark doorways as we drove around the city. Three children who still had a mother that cared were clustered around her in a pile on the sidewalk as they slept, ignored by the people hurrying by. They made a tiny, pathetic pyramid of humanity.

You can't ignore the *gamines* of Bogota. Out of our hotel room, we could see a beautiful public fountain that graced the cobbled square just across the street. We could also see the little dusky bodies, naked, that splashed in the cool water in an effort to rid themselves of the layers of grime they accumulated as they lived and slept on the streets. At night, outside the five-star Tecendamah Hotel, a dozen or so kids hustled drivers for the right to look after their cars as they savored the delights of the glitzy restaurants and bars. It was like paying the fox to look after the chickens.

We set up our camera outside our hotel and watched the *gamines* ply their trade. With eyes like raptors, they missed nothing. The corner of a silk scarf revealed itself from the trunk of a Mercedes. In seconds, a boy of about twelve had peeled the scarf from its hiding place. It would fetch a few pesos on the street.

Ward had come from the United States, largely at his own expense, supported only in part by a small fund-raising organization, to help as many of these children as he could. His reasons were simple. "I like kids. I've photographed children all over the world, street children, urchins. I look in their eyes

21

and I see my own two children. So now I want to do something in my life for them, and I came here to Bogota to do it."

Living in a little one-room apartment in the center of the city, Ward spent his days ranging for miles along its streets and alleys, literally looking for trouble. He didn't have to look far. On a dismal downtown side street, he introduced us to two of the wickedest looking villains I'd ever seen.

Their dark eyes had pupils that were reduced to pinpoints from drug use. They were unshaven, and their hands and faces were ingrained with dirt. I anxiously checked that our equipment was close to our feet. I had never been face to face with such a pair of thieves as this. Twenty-year-old Jose Castelena was dressed in a pair of jeans, a suit coat, and turtleneck sweater. The clothes were of such good quality and so filthy that they obviously had a history that predated Jose. His partner, who proudly posed alongside Jose, was named Alphonso Marriela, but Ward said he only answered to the name Diablo, or Devil. Diablo wore a beautifully cut, pinstripe, three-piece suit with a T-shirt underneath. It too was filthy dirty. Neither boy wore shoes.

"They have to steal. They steal to survive. They steal to eat. They steal for support." Ward talked alternately in fluent Spanish to the youths and in articulate English to our camera as he tried to dress Jose's arm. He told us that Jose had been sniffing gasoline to get high and had been smoking at the same time. The resulting fire and explosion had barbecued the underside of his left arm. No hospital would let this disreputable character in its doors, so his only hope was the curbside kindness Ward could provide. Reaching into the large brown canvas bag he carried everywhere with him, Ward took out simple first aid supplies that helped him treat the hundreds of bruises, stab wounds, and burns he saw every day. Jose grimaced and winced, mostly, I thought, for the benefit of our camera, as Ward spread salve onto the raw wound with a tongue depressor. "They steal for sport, and they steal to pay the extortion levied by the city police." Ward Bentley gestured with the ointment-covered depressor at a scruffy youngster in the group that was tightly packed around us. "The police came along and hit him in the head with a billy club, and I have to treat him."

The affection that Ward had for these boys was evident from the tenderness of his actions and his words when he spoke to them. He asked them a question in Spanish, and Jose growled, "Papa. Papa Gringo." This is what these kids from all over Bogota called this strange American who wandered bravely in their midst, Papa Gringo.

I had seen enough by now on these mean streets to understand that the problem was way beyond anything one American Good Samaritan could do. "What hope do these kids have?" I asked. Ward tousled the greasy hair of Diablo. "None," he answered. "They have none." We asked him where these kids slept, and he told us that most found shelter in back alleys. He showed us dumpsters where it was obvious someone had bedded down among the trash the night before. Even on busy avenues, little bodies lay against the fence under the posters advertising movies that they would never see. But some had regular lairs from which they ranged each day to beg or steal and to which they returned in the early hours of the morning when there weren't enough victims about to make staying up longer worthwhile.

On the corner of a busy intersection stood an unfinished building, unfinished for so long it seemed abandoned, neglected, dead. Ward went first. Grasping a metal grating with both hands he "limbo'd" under it to gain access to the home of some of his charges. We climbed a series of cement stairs in the half-dark dampness, our steps ringing with a hollow, forlorn sound against the concrete block walls. We stepped onto the second floor into a puddle of water that lapped against a metal cup lying on its side. From around a brick corner, a trio of youngsters, none older than fifteen, cautiously appeared. Ward put his arm around one boy dressed in a coat made from a burlap bag. They talked together in Spanish, and turning to respond to my question, Ward said, "Sure they steal. They steal gold necklaces, watches, and earings—to eat." He gestured toward his mouth in the Latin fashion. "But no, they are not a threat. They are not a danger. They don't go for tourists with knives and hurt them they way our gangs do in New York City or Chicago or Washington." He placed his hands affectionately on the boy's shoulder, and they smiled at each other fondly, as if sharing some secret that we couldn't possibly understand. "They are not dangerous kids, not at all." As a punctuation mark at the end of his little speech, Ward clasped the homeless boy to his chest.

As we had talked, half a dozen other kids had drifted into this clammy cell of a place they called home. A young girl commenced washing her hair, using a long hose that was illegally connected to some unsuspecting nearby business's water supply. As she hung her head over her chest to prevent the water running down her clothes, her breast dropped out of her skimpy top. There was no privacy for the street kids of Bogota, but they had an instinctive need to stay as clean as they could.

"The police think I sell dope or buy stolen goods, and that's nonsense," said Ward as we stood to take our leave. "What they can't understand," he said, "is that I don't want anything out of this other than a hundred smiles a day, and that's what I get."

Ward told us his simple philosophy. It was that each of us is parent to every child. He lived by that credo against all the odds, until he died of a heart attack in the Dominican Republic in 1988. He was there to take care of the street children. They called him Papa Gringo.

KING OF THE WORMS

LESS THAN TWO hundred and fifty people live in Amherst Junction, Wisconsin, but small as it is, the little town boasts its own royal family. Well, not exactly a family, but a one-man autocracy called George Schroeder. George, who was seventy-two when we met him in 1983, ruled over a unique kingdom with millions of subjects. You see, George is the self-styled "Worm King" of the United States, if not the world.

The long white building on the edge of Amherst Junction had a huge sign on the roof that proclaimed it as a worm haven.

We found George watering a row of white trays, each about eight inches deep. He told us he had been retired for years. So he was no longer in "business," he was in "research." "I run the largest research laboratory in the world, and I work with more than two million worms!" he claimed with great pride.

We gazed around the spotlessly clean building at tray after tray of wriggling masses of worms. The only odor was the musty tang of freshly turned earth. The bright fluorescent lights made it simple for us to follow George as he scurried back and forth between the lines of racks that held his charges.

A man of average height, George carried himself erect and, perhaps because he knew we were coming with the cameras, was dressed in a smart red shirt and black slacks. His thinning hair was snow white offset by the black of his horn-rimmed glasses. His eyes shone with the enthusiasm of the true, gentle fanatic as he held forth of the glories of worms. "The idea is to produce a healthier, more colorful, livelier, and better conditioned earthworm. So once you put this worm on a hook, it will wriggle like crazy to attract fish."

And it appeared George was well on the way to producing a night crawler that would bring tears of joy to the eyes of any fisherman. Digging his large, well-worn hands into a tray of dark, rich, damp peat, George came up with a handful of the largest worms we'd ever seen. They were more like snakes, really, huge segmented creatures that coiled around each other in their blind efforts to cover themselves with their neighbors in the absence of their usual blanket of earth.

We were speechless, which was just as well because George was reaching full flight in his discourse on his subjects. "I'm looking for a superworm, and I think "Herman the Worm" is a superworm," he said. Herman, he told us, was a two-inch weakling when he took him out of shipment ten years before. "I put him on a special diet of carbohydrates, protein, and vitamins. And he grew and grew and grew."

George stared at me with great intensity, not daring me to disbelieve him but just with the sheer force of his conviction. This man was into worms. "And he grew and he grew, and I'd take him on TV shows all over the United States."

On a square of red fabric, this huge worm called Herman happily squirmed around, expanding and contracting under George's caresses. Herman was at least a foot long at full stretch. One end of this gigantic slitherer pulsated and flattened out like a cobra about to strike. They were a team, Herman the humongous worm and George the human enthusiast.

But there was more. Among the millions of worms under George's care was a special species that he claimed had a unique talent—they danced. "We call it a disco dancing, prancing, dancing hula-hula worm," he rattled off. Sure enough, a handful of this exotic species of southern worms leapt into gyrations of wriggles as soon as they were dumped in a heap on the table top. Individuals that had broken loose from the mass performed their own solos, rhythmic leaps and spins, reaching up with their heads, or tails, who knows with a worm.

George beamed with pride. Happiness radiated from him like light from the sun. A true eccentric, this man spent seven days a week quite alone in his laboratory on the edge of an unknown town in Wisconsin. He was happy in his work but delirious with delight when someone listened to his ideas. He said he had been on Johnny Carson many years before, and many newspapers had run feature stories about his work. But until we came along that winter day in 1983, it had been many years since anyone had stopped to listen. It was a big day for George.

There was no aspect of worms that George had overlooked. He was well aware that his charges were one hundred percent protein. "I say to the fishermen, use a nice worm on your hook, and if you don't catch a fish, you can always eat the bait!"

Most people consider man's best friend to be the dog, but not George. "Oh, I love 'em. I just love 'em. I could do this day and night, more research and study and study. I'm learning something every day about 'em."

POWER AT LAST

WHEN JOSEPH BRIDEL returned from the Civil War in 1865, he built his homestead deep in a coulee not far from the Mississippi River near La Crosse, Wisconsin.

Nothing fancy, just a clapboard three-room affair on a hill overlooking the fields he hoped to clear and farm. They sunk a well and found good water, and he and his wife settled down to raise a family.

When we turned off the highway in 1987, we saw a sign that said:

Bridel Coulee

Although more than 120 years had gone by since Joseph Bridel had driven his team in here, not much had changed except for the blacktop road that wound into the valley and the cleared fields scattered among the pines.

Joseph's old house looked about the same. Even an untrained eye could tell that not a lot of modernization had gone on around here. But something had been added. A power pole, freshly turned dirt around its base showing its recent planting, stood stark and awkward looking about ten feet from the southeast corner of the old house.

We had come to Bridel Coulee because this house was the last one in the region to get electricity. The power company said they had installed the wires just a few weeks before our arrival.

Cameraman Phil Thiesse and I were a little nervous as we pounded on the oak plank door. We were coming unannounced, a very unusual thing for us to do. But in this case we had no choice—there was no phone in Joe's house.

The door was opened by a woman. Sixty-nine-year-old Roseena was Joseph Bridel's granddaughter. She pulled her old woolen shawl around her shoulders and eyed us suspiciously. "What do you want," she murmured in a German accent that was surprisingly strong.

It was tough explaining to this simple woman why the people that watched KSTP would be interested in the installation of electricity in a remote old house deep in a coulee in southern Wisconsin. With a lot of smiles and assurances we meant no harm, we managed to get a hesitant invitation to step inside and talk to her brother.

Robert, who we discovered was seventy-seven, was sitting by the only window smoking a cigar. There seemed to be only one room, but a door in the corner led, we were told by Roseena, to where she slept. Robert slept on a bed that was standing in the corner opposite the window.

They didn't say a word. In the vacuum I spluttered along, trying to justify our breaking into the privacy they so obviously treasured. "What conveniences do you have?" I asked. They looked at me as though I were a man from Mars. "What do you mean, conveniences?" asked Robert, lighting another cigar.

I looked up at the dark brown ceiling that once was white but had taken on a murky patina from untold numbers of Robert's smokes. "Well, do you have running water?"

Robert just grunted with disgust, but his sister said, "We have a pump out in the yard." "I suppose you use an outhouse, then?" I said. Roseena looked down at her clasped hands in her lap. I didn't realize why, but my questions were embarrassing her.

"We had an outhouse but it blew down in a storm. We use the bucket." With a slight inclination of her head, Roseena pointed out a covered bucket that stood by the door.

At least, now, they had electricity. "The fifteenth of September was the first time we put the lights on," Robert said as he relit his stogie, which had gone out in the excitement. "It was quite a day, wasn't it?" I asked. Roseena giggled like a little girl as her big brother said, "Yeah, it was so bright we couldn't hardly see." "What do you mean?" I asked.

They both laughed. Things were warming up. I was beginning to think they had not only begun to accept these two curious strangers that had come into their lives but were starting to enjoy themselves. "It was so bright," they said in unison. "With the lamp we were so happy in the dark," said Robert.

Having power at their fingertips hardly changed this couple's lives. We watched Roseena prepare lunch for the two of them on the old wood stove that provided most of the heat and all of their cooking facilities. A can of soup.

There was nothing subtle about the new light in the old homestead. A large flourescent light, starkly white against the brown ceiling, was the only fixture. It lit the room badly. No wonder the two residents mourned the loss of their old kerosine lamp. "Never bothered us," said Robert. "Never bothered us, never thought of it," echoed his sister.

We learned it had taken years of soul-searching consideration before the elderly couple caved into their neighbor's demands that they put in electricity. It made sense if only for the reliable heat it could give their old bones. Both of them were too tired these days to get out of bed several times a night to stoke up the stove.

When it came to the crunch, however, it was not a joint decision. "Well, he's the boss," said Roseena deferentially. "So who made the decision?" I asked. "Well, he did really," she said.

The coming of electricity to this last household did not mean a flood of gadgets were on their way. "No, we don't want that." Roseena was adamant that they were not at all tempted to rush out and buy a television, toaster, or hair dryer. "We don't need it really," she said with a finality that brooked no argument.

It was Robert, of course, who had the last word on the unexpected shock that their sudden rush into the twentieth century had brought them. "You know," he said, "we just got our first bill. This little bit of light and little bit of heat costs us seventy-seven dollars and eighty-five cents."

ALVERA

THE POPULATION OF Zumbrota, Minnesota, is only about two thousand, but every one of them knows Alvera Lohman. Most of them know the details of the story Alvera told us one day, the first time she had ever allowed any media to take photographs of her.

"I was at work, it was about three o'clock in the afternoon, and suddenly I thought I was coming down with the flu." Within a few short hours, Alvera found she couldn't move her arms and legs. Within a day or two, she was completely paralyzed. Alvera was a victim of a dread, incurable disease called polio. This dramatic change in the young woman's life took place in 1957.

I'd heard of Alvera over the years. Nothing specific. Just scraps of information about a remarkable woman who had been in a hospital bed somewhere in Minnesota for a very long time. Then one day I saw a newspaper story that told of a change in federal regulations that meant bedridden patients who were stable had to be moved out of hospital beds and placed in long-term care facilities like nursing homes.

Alvera fell into that category with a bang. She had been in the same little hospital in Zumbrota since shortly after she had contracted polio more than thirty-one years ago. The newspaper story told of Alvera's plight, and it made it quite clear she didn't want to be moved.

As I sat reading the out-of-town newspaper in my office at KSTP, I knew it was time to track down Alvera Lohman. There was story to be told that I thought would interest our viewers, and at the same time I recognized that the wide publicity we could generate could only help this woman stay in her little hospital if she wanted to.

I called the Zumbrota Community Hospital and, much to my surprise, I was put through straight away to Alvera Lohman. Her voice had a strange, high-pitched sound to it because speaking takes a special effort when someone is paralyzed from the neck down. But yes, she would allow us to come and visit her at the hospital and, although I didn't realize at the time this was a breakthrough, she would allow our camera to take her picture.

Cameraman Phil Thiesse and I were not sure what to expect. Even after many years in the television news business, we always feel a little uncomfortable hauling our lights and camera equipment into hospital rooms. After all, not only are these places where people endure all kinds of suffering but they are also their bedrooms.

Walking into Alvera Lohman's sunny room was different. Although she was lying, propped up by several pillows, in bed, it was like she was sitting almost regally in a big chair. She was radiant. She looked years younger than her chronological age of sixty.

Her bright and alert eyes followed our every move as we set up the camera and clipped a tiny microphone to her blue bed jacket. "What exactly is the problem, Alvera?" I asked in my best bedside manner. "After having been here this long," she replied, "I just don't understand why they want me to leave."

Alvera did understand that she wasn't sick anymore in the sense that she needed medication or treatment. But she was, and always would be, totally dependent on a small respirator that did her breathing for her. Her ability to move was restricted to tiny movements of her head, which enabled her to operate a mechanism that turned the pages of the magazines she loved to read.

But these weren't the reasons Alvera wanted so much to be allowed to stay where she was. "This is my hometown," she said. "This is where I know a lot of people, and I get good care here. What more could I ask for?"

Tears welled up in this beautiful woman's eyes. And swallowing a lump like a golfball in my own throat, I pressed on with what I hoped would be gentle questions. "What are the alternatives?"

It turned out there was only one nursing home in town, conveniently located just across the tree-lined street from the hospital. But it was full. There was a waiting list. There would be no bed there for Alvera for at least a year.

So if the law prevailed, Alvera would be wrenched from the environment she called home for more than thirty years and shipped out of town.

The repercussions flowed like ripples through the small community. Alvera's eighty-seven-year-old mother, Esther, walked every day, snow, rain, or shine, the seven or eight blocks from her apartment to the hospital. It was obviously a primary reason this elderly woman stayed so active.

In fact, the whole town cared very much about Alvera. Over the years, she had made connections with all facets of the community. High schoolers would come and talk to her about

35

the problems they faced growing up. Local clergy, of all denominations, would visit because it was such a pleasure and to reaffirm their belief in the resilience and inherent goodness of the human race. There was a constant stream of people, all hours of the day, into that friendly room at Zumbrota Community Hospital. And, of course, there was the staff.

Hospital social worker Elsie Saugen thought that moving Alvra could be a tragic mistake. "It will be absolutely devastating because this is her home. We are family to her, and she thinks of us as family. It would be like uprooting someone from their family."

The whole town was well aware of the predicament that their favorite citizen was in. Many had contacted their political representatives; others had signed petitions.

"No one asked them to do it. But they wanted to do it because they knew Alvera wanted to stay here so bad." Alvera's mother was very agitated as she talked to us on the grassy median outside the front of the hospital. "Everyone knows that the care she has been getting all these years is so good, and no other place could give it to her."

Zumbrota's mayor, Al Collinge, put it in a nutshell: "I want, and I speak for the citizens of the community, I want Alvera to be kept here."

The pleas to the politicians didn't fall on deaf ears. Local Independent Republican Representative Bob Waltham led the charge. "If people know Alvera, they love Alvera," he said. "She's a terrific lady, one of a kind. The whole community is involved with her. It would be a real trauma to take her out of that situation. When you can talk to her and see the tears just start rolling out of her eyes, you just can't help get involved."

Back at the hospital room that Alvera called home I asked her what would happen to her if she was forced to leave. "How do we know? How do we know?" she replied "For you it could be a matter of life and death, couldn't it?" I asked. She replied through her tears, "Could be, could be."

Since it was the law that said Alvera had to be moved, the law had to be challenged. And so it was. The Minnesota State Legislature was persuaded to pick up the costs of Alvera's care, costs that up until then the federal government had been paying.

"It is not often that we pass a bill that benefits only one person." Independent Republican Senator Lyle Merkins of Red Wing had the floor. "But Alvera Lohman is not an ordinary person." The bill passed without argument.

"You are a constant source of inspiration and courage and spiritual motivation to this community and all of Minnesota, and it's our pleasure to identify today, the fourth of May, as Alvera Lohman Day in the state of Minnesota." Lieutenant Governor Marlene Johnson was reading from an impressive scroll in Alvera's room, which was packed with well-wishers.

Alvera shone with happiness. "I didn't expect anything like this. I am so grateful to everyone in Minnesota," she said. "Now I know I can stay here. In my hometown."

PETER IN A PITH
HELMET

MINNESOTA STATE HIGHWAY 60 used to run smack through
the middle of the town of Mountain Lake in the southwest of
the state. But they built a bypass, and Mountain Lake nearly
died. More than six hundred cars an hour used to pass by, and
many used to stop at the little gas station on the corner of the
first intersection at the northeast end of town.

The little white building with the strange red stripe running
around the stucco has been there a long time. In fact, it was old
when the current owner bought it over fifty years ago. It still
is an odd-looking building, with its high chimney at the front
and its peaked doorway. Like a house really, perhaps an elf's
home, friendly and cute. The three gas pumps out front seem
incongruous, just like the owner and operator, Peter Falk.

"Man, you put in time in one of these places if you want to
be a success." Spoken by a man who says he knows what he's
talking about. Eighty-year-old Peter Falk has been dispensing
gas and hot air on this corner since 1937.

Even before cameraman Rich Rumppe and I arrived at this backwater of Minnesota, I knew what we were up against. I'd read a local newspaper feature story about this garrulous old man who had been a fixture on this corner for so long. "I'll hang a remote microphone on him as soon as we get there," I said to Rich. "Then just keep the camera rolling and record everything he says."

Peter Falk was a picture. Baggy pants held up by the widest suspenders I'd ever seen, blue and white checkered shirt showing a large V of long underwear at the neck and a battered eyeglass case leaning precariously out of the pocket. All this topped off by a large, grubby pith helmet.

The pith helmet, one of those supposed-to-be white hard hats with a brim that old-time explorers used to wear, is Peter's trademark. "Buy them half-dozen at a time," he said. "Folks wouldn't recognize me if I didn't have my helmet on."

No one around Mountain Lake can remember when Peter Falk wasn't selling gas on this corner. In fact, a lot of people recall that he's been known to sell all kinds of things. But more about that later.

"Since more than fifty years ago I got one original customer left." Then, with an air of complete finality, "The rest of 'em are dead." Not a man to mince words, our Peter. Nor a man to withhold his opinion. As he leaned against the nickel pop machine that stood, defying time, in the cluttered lobby of the gas station, Peter told tall tales and true about the old days.

"Made good money selling moonshine right here with the gas. They'd drink it right here and take bets on shooting flies off the wall." Our eyes followed his shaking, grease-covered finger to the dozens of bullet holes that peppered the yellowing plaster walls. "We had cheese there, and the flies went for the cheese. Then we knew what we were shooting at." When Prohibition ended, our inventive entrepreneur sold booze legally. "It's a liquid, ain't it?"

40

As we looked around, it became apparent that little had changed around here in fifty years. What looked like the same tired old bottles and cans of indeterminate lubricants stood ignored by drivers of four-wheel-drive pickups just as they never tempted the owners of new Model T Fords. The labels were brown and curling at the edges. Dust and grime added their own dash of character. Fifty-year-old dispensers for windshield-wiper blades and oil stood empty and rusting. On the wall, several calendars documented the passage of time, at least until 1956.

And Peter jawed on. "I remember the great grasshopper plague of 1932. They ate fence posts. They ate everything." We stood our ground. We had been warned we might hear a story or two, so we were ready. After all, this is what we had come for. As he reached for a sealed jelly jar amid the other bric-a-brac on the swaybacked shelf, Peter proceeded with the tale of the great grasshopper plague.

"Drove down south to see for myself," he said, lighting another cigarette from the one he had just smoked to a finger-singeing butt. "Had to get outa there fast. The lousy critters started to eat the cloth top of my new car." One eye peered at me from a crinckled face. I smiled but didn't laugh. I didn't know if he was serious or pulling my leg. If I had any doubts about how big the grasshoppers were in 1932, Peter was about to put them to rest.

"See here if you don't believe me," he said as he banged down a jelly jar with a thump on the old mahogany counter. "I pulled the wings off that one so he couldn't get away from me." As the camera zoomed in to try to define the contents of the murky jar, my eyes did the same. Sure enough, there was a huge grasshopper, minus its wings, floating in a sepia liquid. Peter was just warming up. "You should have seen the ones that got away—as big as sparrows."

Peter suddenly stopped trying to impress his visitors from

41

the cities. He was out of cigarettes. "Been a steady smoker for sixty-nine years. It's good for my heart." It soon became apparent how this unusual man could afford to smoke so much. The one modern touch in this museum of a gas station was the cigarette machine. "Inexpensive too," said Peter as he wielded a big bunch of keys, snapped open the machine, and helped himself.

Before they opened the new highway, hundreds of cars stopped at Peter Falk's little business every day. Now it's down to a trickle. Peter is eighty-two, last we heard, and still pumping gas. A few regulars still come by to get a fill and hear the latest story, or an old one told again with the kind of relish only an expert can give it.

Peter still spurns the ancient till abandoned on the counter inside. He takes the bills and dances a little jig that bounces up a handful of change into his hand from his pants pockets, which must surely bottom out around his knees.

So if you're bound southwest on Minnesota State Highway 60 towards Worthington, it's worth taking the old road to get your gas in Mountain Lake from Peter Falk if for no other reason than he's always a penny cheaper than the competition.

SAVE THE WHALES

I HAD ONLY been back in the office for about thirty minutes and was still writing a story that we were producing about a member of the Minnesota Orchestra who had become very ill. Jack Moore was a timpanist, and we knew him from a segment we had produced, with his help, about a walk he had taken once in the Snowy Mountains of eastern Australia. Subsequently, Jack had been struck down with a massive brain tumor and now was unable to participate in life as we all know it. His many friends in the Minnesota Orchestra had stood by Jack throughout his ordeal, and in the next few days, they were to give their services freely to raise money for Jack's care. This is the story I was working on this October day in 1988.

Not for the first time in my life, and most likely not for the last, a day that had begun quite routinely was about to burst into a great adventure. When the phone on my desk gave a single ring, I knew it was a call from within the building. I recognized the voice of assignment editor Robin Smythe as

43

she said four words that started an incredible process: "Let's go to Alaska."

I have to back up here and explain that early in October 1988, three whales were found trapped in the fast-forming sea ice near Barrow, Alaska. The three California grey whales were on their annual migration south and somehow found themselves too close to shore and trapped by the rapidly forming ice.

Local hunters had found them and alerted the authorities. They were not the eating kind of whales for the Eskimos of the region, so a small effort was begun to keep the breathing hole in the ice open.

A story published in the Anchorage paper was syndicated around the country, and within a week, the first television pictures were being shown on the networks. We were all aware of this dramatic story, but short of a local angle, we were relegated to being viewers, just like everyone else.

I thought at one point we did have an angle on this story when a young man named Rick Skluzacek, from Lakeland, Minnesota, called me and said a company his father owned produced a machine that could keep the breathing holes open for the whales. Rick wanted to know if KSTP's owner, Stanley Hubbard, would be prepared to fly one of his corporate aircraft up to Barrow to deliver Rick and his machines. I told Rick to call Mr. Hubbard's office, and thinking this was a real long shot, I forgot about it. I had underestimated Stanley's sense of adventure and his generosity.

"Let's go to Alaska." That was all she had said. But I knew things would happen fast, and I hurriedly put the finishing touches on the script about the orchestra's benefit for Jack Moore.

At Holman Field, St. Paul's downtown airport, pilots Morgan Combs and Ken Speer were preparing Stanley's Grumman aircraft for the three-thousand-mile flight to Barrow. It's a big airplane. Fitted out for comfort rather than economy, it seats about a dozen people on couches or large, very comfortable reclining chairs. Its two huge Rolls Royce turboprop engines were capable of getting us to Barrow with only one stop for fuel. Food for the journey was being rushed from the caterers. Flight plans were being constructed and filed with the FAA. And both Morgan and Ken were racing around trying to scrape together as much cold-weather clothing as they could.

As I pounded the typewriter, a helicopter was in the air bound for the heliport on the roof of KSTP on University Avenue in St. Paul. I took a second or two to call my wife, Amanda, and told her, not for the first time in our lives, "Pack all my cold-weather gear. I'm leaving immediately."

I finished the orchestra script, recorded the narration, and gave some hasty directions to the editor. In the meantime, the office staff of KSTP had produced money for expenses for myself, cameraman John Elliot, and producer Jean Bumgardner. Once the decision had been made that we would fly our own aircraft to Barrow carrying twenty of the bubble-making machines made by Casco Marine of Lakeland, Minnesota, and a news crew, our organization went into high gear.

There was no time to lose. First and foremost, we now knew the machines were considered critical to the whales' survival. Rick Skluzacek and his brother-in-law Greg Ferrian were already in Barrow, having paid their own fares to get there. The two machines they had taken with them were an immediate success, and the whales were, for the time being, safe from drowning. Secondly, the story had assumed astronomical proportions. The papers were full of the effort to save the three California grey whales. All three networks now had crews at the scene, and it was a major story every night on the news.

"The helicopter will be on the roof in ten minutes." Robin reminded me that the chopper was coming to pick me and Stanley Hubbard's son Robbie up to take us home for our gear. Both Robbie and I live not far from the St. Croix River, he on the Minnesota side and I on the Wisconsin side. Robbie, as adventurous as his father, was coming with us. Not just to watch us work, but to help where he could and, what turned out to be very important to us later, to provide protection with his heavy-duty hunting rifle. "Chopper's on the roof—off you go."

Despite her years of experience assigning newspeople like myself to all kinds of strange places, Robin was as excited as anyone else in the newsroom that day. "Good luck," she yelled as we shot up the stairs that led to the roof.

We dropped Robbie off at his riverside home first. "We'll pick you up in about fifteen minutes," I said as the pilot gunned the jet engine and we lifted off toward the river. Amanda is used to me suddenly taking off for parts unknown at a minute's notice, but this was the first time I had come home for my clothes in a Jet Ranger. As we circled my house in the country north of Hudson, Wisconsin, I could see her and our collie, Mac, standing by the house. And when the helicopter hovered over the grassy area at the back, I was delighted to see millions of leaves blown right into the surrounding woods. "That's one job you've saved me," I yelled to the pilot on the intercom that was integrated into the headsets we both wore.

I rushed into the house and quickly changed from the more formal clothes I had been wearing only an hour before at Orchestra Hall into some comfortable jeans and a sweat shirt. I knew from experience that when faced with long plane journeys, fashion should take second place to comfort. "I've packed everything I think you'll need," said Amanda. She had, too. I grunted as I hefted the large canvas bag I use to carry my winter work clothing. No time for niceties or long good-byes. A quick hug and a kiss and I was down the slope to the helicopter, which was waiting with its engine still running.

As I clambered into the seat beside the pilot, I saw my three youngest children, eight-year-old Jeremy, twelve-year-old Jessica, and thirteen-year-old Verity, come running down the driveway toward the house. They gaped with astonishment as they came around the corner to see this huge helicopter with their father at the window lift off in a flurry of fallen leaves. Off on another adventure. The kids, I knew, were excited but not unduly surprised. All their lives they had seen their father come and go, and they only knew what he was up to from the stories they watched on the news each night.

There was a flurry of activity at the airport as we prepared to leave. My colleague Kevyn Burger was there with a camer-aman to record our departure, and she was preparing to do a live report on the five o'clock news, which was due to begin in a few minutes. People were hauling clothing and supplies aboard the plane, and the twenty Casco Marine bubblers were being double-checked before being stowed in the baggage compartment. Word of this extraordinary flight of mercy had attracted a large group of curious people, who stood around watching our antics on this sunny fall day in Minnesota.

Only a couple of hours after the decision to go, we were off to the United States' most northern point, a tiny town called Barrow more than three thousand miles north of the twin cit-ies of Minneapolis and St. Paul. After the initial flush of ex-citement wore off, it became a tedious journey, broken only by a short stop in Edmonton, Alberta, for fuel and a curious once-over by Canadian customs and a five-hour break for some real "bed sleep" in a motel in Fairbanks, Alaska.

It was midmorning in Barrow when our plane touched down. The temperature was fifteen degrees below zero, and there was a stiff breeze from the north. Morgan taxied the

Grumman up to the only large hanger at the airport, the door of the aircraft opened, and the cold came in.

We had no idea what to expect. Because of our hurried departure, I had had no opportunity to make phone calls to set up contacts or even find out where the whales were. I knew that Robin had been busy making sure we all had accommodations in Barrow. A radio message to the plane had informed us that we were placed at various private homes in the arctic town. Every hotel room in the place was full of newspeople. Robin, bless her heart, had also arranged rental of a big pickup truck, which was to provide us with plenty of excitement. But more about that later.

As luck would have it, we arrived at the right place at the right time. Inside the huge hanger that belonged to the North Slope Borough, the governing body for this huge slice of Alaska, was the daily meeting. Actually, the meeting, of the local officials, Alaska National Guard officers, biologists, helicopter pilots, and oil company technicians, was upstairs in a suite of offices. Downstairs it was a zoo.

Dozens of newspaper and television people from all over the world milled around, waiting to determine what the next move would be in the effort to save the whales and, most importantly for us, who would be the lucky ones who would get to ride the official helicopter out onto the ice.

"Are you the guys that have brought the bubblers?" The enquiry came from a bear of a man with a blue uniform on that identified him as an employee of the borough. He was excited to learn we were indeed the carriers of the Casco bubblers and assured us that we, and the machines, would soon be on our way to save the whales. So, with all the others, we waited.

"Excuse me, who are you?" This enquiry came in clipped British tones from a well-dressed man who had popped out of the crowd. I explained that we were from KSTP-TV and that we had brought the bubblers. "No, I mean who *are* you?

48

I was in Houston, Texas, covering the latest space shuttle mission a few weeks ago, and I saw you there. Then I returned to my home in New York and saw you on a national television show called "Incredible Sunday," and here you are in Barrow, Alaska." I explained to David Foster from Britain's TV AM that I had been so active because of my work at KSTP, and I'm happy to say we became good friends.

As we waited, an impromptu basketball game had broken out among the network cameramen using a ball made up of the sticky, useful-for-all-things gaffers tape that they all have plenty of. Suddenly, a bearded man swept up to me who I hadn't seen since we had been at the north pole two years before.

I was in luck. Geoff Carroll, who had been part of the Will Steger team that had conquered the pole by dogsled in 1986, was one of the biologists in charge of the welfare of the three trapped whales. Geoff assured us that he would be available to us at any time for interviews and information, and he returned to the everlasting meeting upstairs. But my surprises were not over.

"Aren't you Jason Davis?" The voice was distinctly Australian, that much I recognized, but the face escaped me. "My name's Ken Burslem. We used to work together at Channel Nine. Don't you remember?" It was no wonder I had trouble with my memory. In the middle of this chaotic scene, here was a man who I hadn't seen since my days as a television reporter at Channel Nine in Melbourne, Australia, seventeen years before. It's a small world. Especially when a big story is afoot.

I may have been among friends within minutes of my arrival in Barrow, but as we waited, it became apparent that as late arrivals, despite the earlier assurances of the man in the blue uniform, we were at the bottom of the list for a ride out to the whales on the borough helicopter.

I was bemoaning our fate to a newspaper reporter from Anchorage when he came up with a bit of information that gave us an edge on the competition for days. "You can drive out to the whales, you know," he said. I was skeptical. "Why would all these media people impatiently wait for the helicopter if you could get out there by road?" "What road?" my new-found best friend said. "You have to drive across the ice."

Well, this was music to my ears. Coming, as we did, from Minnesota, driving on the ice was almost second nature to us. I could readily understand why, even if they knew it was possible, media people from Los Angeles, New York, Australia, or Japan would consider a helicopter the only practical way out onto the frozen Arctic Ocean.

Robbie Hubbard walked into the cavernous hanger, having just delivered our editing equipment to the Top of the World Motel, where they had kindly let us use their tiny staff lounge as a makeshift studio. "Let's go, Robbie," I said, grabbing a box containing one of the bubblers we had brought up from Minnesota. Cameraman John Elliot grabbed another, and we threw them in the back of the big old pickup truck we had rented. Our camera equipment was already in the back of the cab, so we were on our way within seconds.

With our newspaper reporter colleague as a guide, we zoomed through the center of Barrow and headed out along the coast. At first, I thought it was going to be easy. The road seemed to head straight toward the point that marked the land nearest to the trapped whales. But after about five miles, it was obvious that only a Caterpillar tractor could go any farther.

We thought about it for a split second only. The snowmobile tracks showed where other engine-powered vehicles had headed for the whales, and we followed them. We were on the ice, but we still had several miles to go. Even with our home state experience, it's still nerve-wracking to drive on strange ice. Particularly when the only tracks in sight are made by snowmobiles. Our truck, a four-wheel-drive monster of a machine, must have weighed fifty times more than any snow machine.

The weather was overcast, and the whole horizon had a milky haze to it that made things difficult to define. If it hadn't been for our newspaper friend, we would never have found the whales. "Park here," he said. "Don't want to get too close."

Too close to what, I wondered. I couldn't see much. A couple of snowmobiles were parked by a shedlike structure that was on huge timber skids. Several Eskimos were moving around, but they ignored us completely.

"Where are the whales?" I asked. "Over there." They pointed at a small knot of people who seemed suspended in space because the sky and the ice were the same color. Amazing. We had come over three thousand miles to see what the whole world was talking about, and just a few paces away, there they were.

Only a stone's throw from the shore, several long channels had been cut in the ice. As we walked up to the one farthest from the land, two whales surfaced almost simultaneously. John began to shoot the scene while I stood transfixed by this extraordinarily close meeting between man and beast. There were quite a few Eskimos watching too. They were, naturally, well aware you didn't need a multimillion-dollar helicopter to see the whales.

I knelt beside the hole in the ice. The three whales were surfacing regularly for air in these man-made leads. I wanted to get as close as I could. The water boiled beside me, and I could see in the depths the thirty-foot body of one of the animals as it came up for breath. Its huge head broke the surface with a whoosh as it first expelled a plug of water then, with a sigh, sucked in air.

I reached out and touched the cold, smooth skin and looked at the unblinking eye that seemed to be returning my gaze. My feelings were of sorrow. I stood up and looked at the ridge on the horizon that marked the edge of the ice and the beginning of the open water. It was so far.

We were aware that herculean efforts had been made to break these animals out of their natural prison before we arrived. The only thing that had been achieved so far was that the whales hadn't drowned. The unflagging work of the Eskimos with chain saws and the two bubbling machines from Minnesota had kept the breathing holes open, but it was many miles to the open sea and freedom.

But we had a story to produce, and I knew that producer Jean Bumgardner back in Barrow would be anxiously waiting for our return. We got back to town just in time to put together our first report from Barrow. It was sent out by satellite and seen by viewers in Minnesota and elsewhere that same night.

From that day on, we followed the efforts to save the whales every day. Unlike our colleagues from the rest of the world's media, we were up at seven every morning, drove to the whales across the ice, and often made it back before the first helicopter lifted out of Barrow.

The second day, one of the whales died. At least it disappeared. Geoff Carroll was sure it had perished. He said it was the smallest, the youngest, and therefore the most vulnerable. But two were still alive, and the project to save them never flagged.

As the days passed, the chain of breathing holes stepped towards the open water, but everyone knew that this effort, by itself, could not save the whales. On the horizon, we could all see a forty-foot barrier that was the huge pressure ridge caused by the moving sea ice grinding up against the land-fast ice. But one evening, an incredible rumor was confirmed: The Russians were coming. For days, there had been reports that a couple of Soviet icebreakers might add their substantial muscle to the endeavor, but there was also a great deal of

52

skepticism that these huge, expensive ships would be relieved of their icebreaking tasks in the Soviet Arctic to travel hundreds of miles to save a couple of wayward grey whales.

The doubters underestimated the impact this unusual story was having around the world. Modern news coverage knows no limits. The hundred or so newspeople working in Barrow represented, through syndication, every newspaper, radio station, and television station in the world. From China to Europe, from South Africa to Siberia, the front pages and the headlines gave daily accounts of what a small band of Eskimos, armed with a handful of electric bubblers from Minnesota, were doing to save the whales.

The Soviet ships were coming to carve a passage through the ice barrier that on a clear day we could see stretching across the horizon like a wall. The experts had been out there by helicopter and pronounced it impenetrable, at least by the chain saws of the Eskimo workers. It soared forty feet in the air, great jagged chunks of ice formed by the same process that created the coastal mountains of the earth itself, the results of an unstoppable mass of floating sea ice meeting the immovable pan of ice that was frozen fast to the land. Soundings showed that in places, it reached down to the sea floor another sixty feet—a hundred feet of ice! I was determined to see this oddity of nature and produce a story about this last hurdle for the whales that was turning this hometown effort into an international cause.

It was not a good day. The skies were overcast, and an offshore wind aggravated the ten-degrees-below-zero temperatures to a wind chill factor of thirty degrees below zero. Visibility was so poor that as we stood beside our rented snowmobile at the edge of the frozen ocean, we couldn't see the pressure ridge four miles or so to seaward. We dressed as warmly as we could. Face masks and goggles were essential. At these temperatures, the speed of the snowmobile would create a chill that would freeze exposed skin in minutes. Robbie was ready to drive, legs astride the rumbling machine, his rifle slung diagonally across his broad back. John faced backwards, tucked with his precious camera into the tiny sled, and I hung on the back with a foot on each runner looking forward into the wind. We were alone. It was early in the morning, and the daily parade of newspeople and local visitors was still a couple of hours away. In the distance, we could see the huddled figures of the faithful Eskimos tending the bubbling machines and working steadily on the next link in the chain of breathing holes. For a second or two, I wondered about the wisdom of venturing out on the virgin ice, where several polar bears had been seen only the day before. Foolishly, I said, "Let's go."

The snow-covered ice was bumpy, and the old snowmobile and its heavily loaded sled made slow, uncomfortable progress. The jangled horizon that was the top of the pressure ridge soon came into view, but it didn't seem to get closer as what seemed like miles passed under the runners of the sled. The sounds we heard under the several layers of masks and hats we wore were just the wind and the tortured scream of the snowmobile engine.

I smelled it first. The pristine air of the Arctic Ocean took on a scorched taint. Something was wrong. I blinked away the tears from my squinted eyes and stared ahead. Through the cloud of powder snow thrown up by the spinning tracks of the snowmobile, I could see the dark shape with the slash of rifle that was Robbie's back. But off to his left there was something else—smoke! I tried to scream out at the top of my voice, but the layers of wool and polypropylene covering my mouth only allowed a muffled grunt to compete with the wind and the engine noise. I tore at the face covering with my mitten-covered hands and was able to yell more effectively at Robbie's stoic back. "Robbie, stop!" I saw him stiffen, and his head screwed around to try and identify the strange sound that had obviously penetrated his head clothing. I waved frantically, and he shut back the throttle, bringing the machine and its following sled to a sudden, shuddering halt.

Obviously, Robbie was still unaware of the emergency, so I galvanized my stiff and frozen legs into reluctant action. Running to the snowmobile, I threw open the hood to find the rubber insulation on the underside in flames. My heavily gloved hands prevented burns as I tore the flaming, inch-thick rubber mat away from the metal housing and threw it onto the snow. The damage was minimal. Confined to just the insulation, it would not inhibit our progress, although we would be louder, a fractional addition to our vulnerability. Polar bears are curious creatures, and they are attracted to anything that moves or makes a noise.

We should have turned back, but we had made a commitment to the producers back in the Twin Cities that we would feed them a story about the pressure ridge for the news that night, and although it still seemed a long way to go to the ridge, we figured we must be at least halfway.

Robbie restarted the machine, John eased back into the sled, and I braced myself for another ordeal of travel. We hadn't gone more than a mile when I imagined I smelled burning again. I shook my head and put it down to the residue of the previous mishap still clinging to my face mask. The odor persisted, but try as I could, I failed to see any trace of smoke from the snowmobile ten feet ahead of me. Then, although the snow machine engine continued its frenzied scream, we stopped. For a second or two, the three of us froze with surprise. A strange tableau, like a photograph: three men on a sled and snowmobile miles from anywhere in the milky light that gave no definition to our surroundings. Then silence. Robbie had flicked the ignition key and broke the spell. I stepped stiffly off the sled runners and walked up to Robbie. "It just stopped," he said, "just quit moving, but the engine's running okay."

One look under the hood of the snowmobile was enough to tell us the worst. The thick rubber drive belt had destroyed itself. The reenforcing cotton thread that had held the rubber together was all that was left. It was wound in a solid mass around the drive pulley, yards of it, tightly packed with no end in sight. This was my first look at the business end of a snowmobile, but it was apparent that we were dead in the water.

The situation was serious. No one knew where we were. We were several miles from where we had left our pickup truck near the shoreline, and the weather was poor and getting worse. We were physically incapable of walking back carrying our equipment, and it would be unthinkable to leave it there. In any case, walking back toward the land would mean we would be facing into the wind, and there was a very real danger of freezing to death.

Without any real hope, I opened the small compartment behind the machine's seat, looking for some kind of tool kit, anything to improve our dangerous situation. We were in luck. Lying among some bits of rope and some rusty nails was a spare drive belt. Now we had a chance, but there was still the mess of threads around the engine pulley. We were saved by the fact that the engine itself was still very hot. I was able to take off my thick outer gloves and work on the pulley with just my thin polypropylene finger covers on. Robbie stood guard, his large-bore, big-game hunting rifle ready to take out any marauding polar bear that came our way. It was extremely comforting to know Robbie was there as I bent to my task, my head and arms buried inside the engine compartment of the machine.

It took nearly an hour to clean out the old belt's remains and fit the rather sloppy, used belt that was the spare. The three of us held our breath as Robbie started the engine and eased open the throttle. At first, nothing happened, but as he gave it more gas, the loose belt tightened across the pulleys and the snowmobile crept forward. Without any discussion, we turned for the shore. We knew we would be lucky to make it back. Any thoughts of shooting videotape of the pressure ridge were gone, and all we considered now was our survival. It was a heart-in-the-mouth journey. Our imaginations created burning smells and shudders of engine failure every inch of the way. Several times, I yelled for Robbie to stop, and we checked the temperature of the belt. It was hot because it was constantly slipping, but it held, and we limped up to our ice-covered truck with mixed feelings.

We were safe, our lives were no longer in danger, but the day had gone and we had failed to produce the promised story on the pressure ridge. There would be some disappointed and possibly angry people back in the newsroom at KSTP. I knew from experience that there would be little interest in the story of why we failed, so I resolved to try to put together a story for them based on the videotapes supplied each day from the network pool material that I knew Jean would have back at our tiny base at the Top of the World Motel. We were delayed even now when, in my haste to get back to work on the pool material, I buried the four-wheeled truck up to its axles in the quicksandlike shore gravel next to the highway, and we had to abandon it and finish the journey back to town in a taxi.

We worked like Trojans to make up for our failure. I wrote a script covering the continuing battle to save the whales, and John hurriedly edited together a summary of the day's events. Jean raced as fast as her legs could carry her to the satellite transmission point at the Barrow cable television studio and managed to persuade someone to transmit our story. It wasn't what we had set out to send them, but it was a tolerable update on this story that the people of Minnesota had such a personal stake in. At KSTP, the ten o'clock news executive producer Gloria McDonough refused to run the piece because it didn't have a shot of me on camera or an interview with anyone in it. Not our best day.

By the time the effort to save the whales was over, there would be 208 holes cut in the ice, stretching over four and a half miles. This massive feat would have failed, however, without some way of keeping the holes open. Temperatures barely topped ten below zero during the day. At night, under clear skies, the mercury plummeted to twenty-five and thirty below. At these extremes, the sea water froze in seconds. In minutes, it was sturdy enough to walk on.

California grey whales are not accustomed to ice. The biologists knew the animals had to have open water to breath or they would drown. It was Rick Skluzacek's bubblers that saved the day and confounded the experts. When Rick and Greg Ferrian had first approached the whale rescuers by telephone, they had gotten the cold shoulder. No one in Barrow could believe that these little machines, made in a converted electrical substation a couple of hundred yards from the banks of the St. Croix River east of St. Paul, could hope to keep the ice from forming in the fast-freezing ocean off the north coast of Alaska.

Confident they had the answer to the dilemma and lacking a response from KSTP, the two brothers-in-law took matters into their own hands. They grabbed a couple of machines out of stock and took the first available flight to Seattle, on to Anchorage, and then to as far as planes fly—Barrow, Alaska.

To give the rescue effort organizers in Barrow credit, as soon as they met Rick and Greg and saw their machines, they immediately flew them out to the whales. Portable generators and lights were hurriedly set up, and the first machine was dropped into the man-made breathing hole. The Eskimo workers watched in amazement as the slush and rubble ice swept to the edges of the hole. The bubbling action created by the little plastic propellor driven by a submersible electric motor was perfect. And what was most surprising was the reaction of the whales.

It was thought the bright lights and the noise of the generators, not to mention the gurgling sound of the bubblers, would frighten the whales and drive them away from the life-saving holes. But as the little group of Minnesotans, biologists, and Eskimos watched the first machine do its job, a huge head rose from the water and actually nuzzled the bubbles pouring from the machine. A ragged cheer went up there on the ice. Now there was hope that these lost and weakening mammals could hold out while a channel to freedom was cut through the ice.

After we had been covering the story for several days, I realized that every time we went out onto the ice, day or night, either Rick or Greg was there. They were so dedicated to saving the whales that they had elected to take twelve-hour shifts tending the machines we had brought from Minnesota, making sure the generators were kept gassed-up and moving all the equipment fifty feet ahead each time the Eskimo workers advanced the series of holes toward the open sea.

One morning at six, we met Greg at the oil company service center where he was staying. It was twenty-five degrees below zero, and he faced twelve hours on the ice with no source of heat, no place even to sit down. The only food he would have would be the snacks he could ram into his parka pockets. We recorded his efforts to start the snowmobile that was encased in ice and snow, the bumpy ride out to the whales, now a couple of miles from shore, and his quiet resignation as he took over from Rick, who had been there all night. This was the kind of dedication we saw all around us, and it was the thrust of our nightly reports back to Minnesota.

By now, the story was a major news event around the

world. Reports that two Soviet icebreakers were on their way to help expanded the interest into the Soviet Union. Every news agency and television outlet on earth was represented in Barrow. We were feeding our material not only to KSTP in the Twin Cities but also through a satellite group called Conus to stations all around the country.

All of the television material was being fed out of the little cable television control room on the ground floor of a small office building in downtown Barrow. It was in use twenty-four hours a day. When it wasn't needed for the United States networks, the teams from Australia were using it. When they were off the air, the BBC and ITV news people from Britian were busy. And then there was us.

We were the only local television station outside Alaska covering this event on a daily basis. We had to squeeze in where we could. Complicating our lot were requests for coverage from other stations around the country linked to us by the Conus network.

As all the television material was being fed out of the local cable television operation, the people of Barrow had a unique opportunity. By tuning the sets in their homes to Channel 22, they could watch television reporters from around the world presenting their pieces to their various organizations.

The way it worked, cables were run out of the building, and each individual TV group hooked up its own camera and placed its reporter in front, with the skyline of Barrow and part of the ice-covered ocean behind. This led to some funny incidents because not only did the people in their living rooms see the edited and cleverly produced news items that the reporters and producers had worked all day to put together, but they were privy to what went on before and after the reporters actually went on the air.

An Australian reporter lost a lot of points locally when just before he went live to Sydney, someone stepped in front of the camera and sprinkled snow and ice on his shoulders. It was the subject of great merriment around Barrow for days.

I was well aware that I was being watched one day as I waited to make a live report to a station in San Francisco. We were having a problem with the audio. They could see me in the control room in San Francisco, but because of a glitch somewhere, they couldn't hear me. I could hear them, and they said, "Keep talking, just keep talking while we try to find the problem."

After about ten minutes of rambling and counting backwards and forwards to ten, I became bored, and knowing well that hundreds of Barrow residents were gleefully watching me make a fool of myself, I began to address them. "I just want to take this opportunity to thank everyone in Barrow for your hospitality toward all of us media types during the whale rescue," I said. I went on to thank personally the two schoolteachers who had kindly provided a room for me during our stay. I told everyone who was watching about where I came from and even how many children I had.

"Keep talking. Keep talking," I heard San Francisco plead in my ear plug. "Well, I don't know what else to tell you folks," I continued lamely. "If I had any kind of voice, I would sing," I rambled on, trying to think of a joke I could tell to an audience consisting largely of Eskimos. Another three or four minutes went by. It seemed like an eternity. I was getting cold standing outside the office building, even under the television lights.

Suddenly, out of the corner of my eye, I saw a kid of about ten years old come racing down the street toward me. "Oh, no," I thought. "That's all I need now, a kid pestering me while I stand by to go live to millions in California." The boy ran right up to me, stopped for an instant to get his breath back, and said, "My Dad says, please sing!"

The next night, we were able to report to the world that the

61

two remaining whales had apparently made it to the open sea. This joint effort of the Eskimos with their chain saws and the awesome power of the Soviet icebreakers had provided a path, and the animals must have taken it. The way was open, and they were nowhere to be seen.

The fate of the two whales will probably never be known for sure, but as biologist Geoff Carroll said to me as we stood looking at the empty, ice-covered ocean, "You can make up your own ending to this story. Me, I prefer to think that after such an effort, the two animals are on their way to the warm healing waters of California."

STANLEY'S STORE

THE LETTER FROM a woman in Redwood Falls, Minnesota, said, "There is an interesting personality in our vicinity by the name of Stanley Petrowski." Well, I get a lot of letters that begin this way, but I read on. "He runs a business and merchandise store that is reminiscent of years gone by." Now we're talking. An interesting man and what sounds like a visually interesting business. "He talks a mile a minute about all kinds of subjects, and he has stock so old that antique dealers shop there." Sold!

A few days later, cameraman Phil Thiesse and I drove down the main street of Wabasso, Minnesota. We didn't need directions to find Stanley's store. It was the only business still open in this town that like so many others we visit on our travels had been hard hit by too many years of tough times for the farmers. Main street Wabasso was deserted.

In recognition of the heat of summer, a small, round, plastic

63

children's wading pool was leaning up against the window of the store that, oddly, had a sign on it saying:

We peered through the milky glass window at displays of hardware products that had obviously been there for years. What would we find inside?

A bell somewhere went ding as we swung the door open, but no one came to see who had come in. Actually, maybe someone did come, but there was no way we could see anyone. At first glance, it looked like an impenetrable wall of merchandise. From floor to ceiling across our entire field of vision ranged the widest variety of goods I'd ever seen in one place. What was amazing was that the stacks seemed to have no visible means of support. The teetering piles of goods were defying gravity.

We were still trying to figure out how to get past this barrier of bargains when Stanley Petrowski shot out of the display like a rabbit out of its hole.

Stanley was a short, tubby man. His open-neck shirt had two pockets. One had one of those plastic protectors in it with a line of multicolored pens and pencils ready to roll. The other pocket bulged heavily. I never did discover what it held. Behind his plastic-rimmed glasses, Stanley's eyes were bright and friendly and, above all, helpful. I guess years of being in business like this had molded the man into a "helpful."

"May I help you?" I knew he was going to say that. Stanley

was delighted that we had come to produce a television feature story about his store. He was flattered, and he was proud—proud of what he had achieved in his sixty-nine years, forty-seven of which he had spent minding his store.

As we became accustomed to the limited light that managed to penetrate the displays, we could see that not an inch was wasted. A man of average build who had come in for a number eight three-quarter-inch wood screw had to turn sideways to move down the cramped aisles. You could lose your entire family in here and not find them for weeks.

There didn't seem to be any method to the way things were laid out. Much of the stock had a layer of dust that betrayed its lack of saleability. A pile of assorted plumbing supplies looked as if no one had touched it for years. Next to the pipes and valves were some baby diapers and a mole trap. We're not talking about one or two items here, we're talking thousands!

"Do you know where everything is?" I asked a beaming Stanley. "You betcha." And to prove it, we had him walk up and down each aisle, along all four walls, and into several alcoves and tell us where things were. "Nails, toilet paper, wallpaper paste, rat poison, window shades, sheet metal screws . . . " I could hear the steady chant of Stanley calling off his stock as he and Phil recorded it for all time. "Record albums, lampshades, drain augers, toothbrushes, six-inch bolts, gravestones . . . " Gravestones! Sure enough, among the bed sheets and backgammon games was a beautifully carved headstone:

FATHER
GERALD A. FREEMAN
1932-1970

No, Stanley wasn't waiting for someone to come by who had a father named Gerry Freeman who just happened to have died in 1970. The stone was a sample that Stanley would show the bereaved who would come by when he was wearing his other hat. Stanley Petrowski was also the town undertaker.

While Stanley may have been short on organization, his self-esteem was boundless. "I designed this store. I made sure I had every bit of space filled in." Then a bit of logic that escaped me. "No sense in heating air, because it'll get cold. This way we got more stuff in. It keeps the place warmer, too." Stanley laughed at the thought of his own cleverness. As he prattled on, my eyes were drawn to a display of kitchen utensils, old kitchen utensils. It was like we had entered a time warp and suddenly found ourselves shopping at a store sometime in the midforties. A card, yellowing with age, proclaimed the product attached was the "Wonder Kitchen Utensil." It looked like an egg beater, and it was, I suppose, a forty-year-old version of a food processor. The price had not changed since Stanley put it on the shelf almost forty years before, $1.95.

Stanley, not at all fazed by my wandering attention, was regaling us with the history of his business. "We used to be on the other side with the implements. We moved to this side in 1952. Everything was clean then. I sold most of the other stuff that was there then, but some of this stuff could be here since then."

Several people had come into the store while we were talking to the proprietor, and the ritual never altered. Stanley knew everyone by first name and knew exactly where, in his jungle of a store, dwelt the item he or she wanted.

Stanley, ever the sharp businessman, was now telling me that despite appearances, there was a good living to be made running a general store. "I feel just like the farmer," he said. "He holds on to his meat, soybeans, grains, and whatnot until the price has gone up, and . . . " Stanley swept his arm across the bewildering vista of stock that overwhelmed his store and said, "A lot of this stuff has doubled up."

My head was swimming with the visual overload that was Stanley's store and the sheer enthusiasm of the man. I had one final question. "Stanley, have you ever had a clearance sale?" He never missed a beat. "Nope, never had to."

Our television piece ended with a gale of laughter. Mine.

MIRACLE OF
MOORHEAD

"HE WAS JUST out of it. He couldn't do anything but just move one eye, just one eye." Gloria Meyer sat in the sun on the tiny porch of her mobile home on the outskirts of Fargo, North Dakota, describing what happened to her sixteen-year-old son, Roger, when a massive growth of blood vessels strangled his brain stem two years before. When Roger suddenly slumped across her kitchen table, the doctors said he had only weeks to live. Gloria, a single mother with other children, one of them mentally handicapped, simply couldn't cope.

But comatose Roger had a friend. David Ortner had been Roger's instructor in a Naval Sea Cadet Corps group that the boy had joined shortly before he became ill.

David, who lived with his mother and ran a small robotics company in Moorhead, Minnesota, heard of Roger's condition and learned that, at best, the boy was facing a lifetime of intensive care in an institution. At worst, he would die without ever regaining consciousness. Only he knows how he pulled it off, but this Good Samaritan, with Gloria Meyer's blessing, managed to persuade the doctors and other authorities that he could and would take care of Roger.

"I wasn't convinced of anything, but there wasn't anything else to do. What do you do? You have seven doctors who say he's never going to get better." As David stood in a room in the basement of his mother's house that he had turned into a homemade intensive care unit, he showed us some of the splints and rigid medical devices that he had to strap onto Roger when the boy would fling himself about dangerously as he suffered coma-induced convulsions.

"When I brought him home, I brought him home to die. His temperature fluctuated between 97 and 107 degrees. We used sixty dollars worth of ice the first thirty days."

We had been attracted to this story because of the remarkable devotion of David Ortner. He showed us a medical log that detailed every minute of Roger Meyer's illness. He told us of his efforts to bring the boy back to a full life by hauling him everywhere he went. He bought a van so that he could take Roger to his lake cabin near Pelican Rapids, Minnesota. Roger would sit slumped in a chair, seemingly oblivious to everything. David was undeterred. He played music for him and talked to him constantly. Several times, the boy nearly died. On one occasion, a police escort had to be used to get him back to the Fargo hospital from St. Paul. He made it with only minutes to spare.

"The first couple of months, he was supposed to be dead, okay? After sixty days, what do you do? He didn't die." David smiled. Anything short of death was a kind of victory for this man who was prepared to give up everything in his quixotic quest for Roger's life. Roger's insurance came up short, and David reached into his own pocket to the tune of more than sixty thousand dollars. After a year and a half had gone by, Roger was still breathing but showed absolutely no response, despite everything David had done. "I used to wake up each morning and check to see if he was still alive, and if he was, it was a good day," David said.

A dozen operations had by now been performed on Roger's skull, and the doctors uniformly told David he was crazy to persist. "They said it was impossible. Well, are those people there to tell us how to die or are they there to give us encouragement to live?"

Eighteen months and three days after David took Roger home, Roger's leg moved. "I said, Roger, if you understand me, raise the leg up. And it bucked right up in the air." David's eyes filled with tears, and his voice broke with the happiness and relief that he could still feel months after this momentous event.

As we produced this story for television, the scene quickly changed to a picture of David at the wheel of a boat. He is looking over his shoulder, and he says, "Okay, Son, get into the water and keep the rope, okay?" The next shot shows Roger Meyer, the miracle boy of Moorhead, gliding along effortlessly at thirty miles an hour on water skis!

"Oh, God, I love him." David was the picture of pride and happiness as he drove the boat all over Pelican Lake. "That's all you've got to do—have some faith and go for it."

As Roger dropped off the skis in the shallows, David brought the boat back to the dock. With his right fist clenched, he threw his arm into the air in a dramatic victory salute and yelled, "Not bad for a vegetable, huh?"

"He's the greatest man in the world." Roger sat drying himself on a bench by the side of the sparkling blue lake. A tall, fair-haired eighteen-year-old with pale blue eyes and big smile, Roger was only too happy to tell us about a man he had hardly known who had lived beside him almost night and day for more than a year and a half. "He's super. He's the nicest, kindest, caringest person. He's my superdad, and I'm his super-son."

71

I had a final comment to share with the viewers of this special story. It was that if all people who were comatose had someone to care for them like David Ortner cared for Roger Meyer, perhaps some of them wouldn't have to spend the rest of their lives lying in a hospital bed.

LAST NEEDLE

THE TINY, GREY-SHINGLED house in the suburbs of Mankato, Minnesota, was a little ragged at the edges. The grass on the lawn was not exactly country-club standard, and the sagging porch looked like it needed the urgent attention of a carpenter.

Stepping onto the stoop taught us a couple of things about the resident. The four-legged walker showed that whoever lived here was old or disabled, or both. And there was a crudely lettered sign that revealed that life went on inside regardless of infirmity or age.

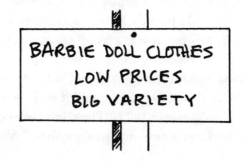

BARBIE DOLL CLOTHES
LOW PRICES
BIG VARIETY

Ninety-two-year-old Gladys Mellor had been making Barbie doll clothes for more than thirty years. I guess that's about from the beginning of children's fascination with the doll.

She made us very welcome, this tiny, vibrant little lady with the silver hair and delicate makeup. She had obviously gone to some trouble with her appearance knowing we were coming to visit her. She had on a deep blue dress with little white flowers all over it. Gladys, except for her age, was almost a Barbie herself.

On a table just inside the front door, which opened directly into her living room, were about twenty-five handmade Barbie dresses. They were meticulously cut and sewn. They were beautiful.

The ball gowns caught our eye first. Brilliant satins with silver lace trim. Sweeping dresses that seen in the lens of the camera seemed to be straight out of a fashion magazine. Only when the camera pulled back did it become apparent that these gorgeous clothes were no taller than six or seven inches.

There was everything the well-dressed Barbie could desire, and every piece had a small square scrap of paper pinned to it. This was Gladys's price-marking system. I took a close look. Not a dress over a dollar seventy-five.

We watched Gladys work. She sat with her back to the wall in one corner of her dining room, hunched over the oldest sewing machine I'd ever seen. It was one of those old black machines with little painted flower designs or decals on the baseplate and uprights. It was a treadle unit, and Gladys's thin legs pumped continuously as she sewed.

The sewing machine, it turned out, was the only thing in the house older than Gladys. She said it was over forty years old when she bought it in 1927. "The salesman said I could get my money back on a new machine anytime," She said. "But of course he's been dead for many, many years now so he never had to live up to his bargain."

The 102-year-old sewing machine was the reason we had come from the Twin Cities to Mankato to see Gladys Mellor. Gladys was on the last needle that would fit this obsolete machine, and word had reached us that without more needles, this priceless woman would no longer be able to make Barbie clothes.

"Oh, they tell me I should have an electric machine. I've never used one. I never thought I'd like one. I'm too old to start over on electricity." So Gladys was on her last needle, and she wouldn't use any other sewing machine. "When you're ninety-two years old and you've got one needle to go, I may not be sewing much longer."

Gladys had tried to find the odd-length, two-inch needles she needed for her faithful old machine. But even a short story in the local paper hadn't brought forward any new supplies.

We took our videotape back to the Twin Cities and produced a short story about Gladys's predicament. The results were astounding. Gladys was showered with needles. Some of them indeed were the old two-inchers she needed, but many were competely wrong.

It didn't matter. Gladys not only got her needles but she became aware that she wasn't forgotten, sitting in her little house in the suburbs of Mankato.

For weeks afterwards I got calls from all over the country. "I have some old sewing machine needles that might fit that old lady's machine." After talking once more to Gladys, I had to tell people she had enough to last her the rest of her life and then some.

Gladys herself wasn't really surprised that people had been so generous. "There is some reason the Lord has let me live to ninety-two years old. And the only reason I can think of is that I make people awfully happy with these Barbie clothes."

ROYE RODGERS

IT WAS ONE of those bright, very cold days in early January as cameraman Don Friedell swung our car into the long gravel driveway that pointed at the house. The tires squeaked on the hard packed snow that covered everything to a depth of several inches. At first glance, the old clapboard house looked deserted. The yellowing white paint was flaking off in long tendrils that fluttered in the bone-chilling wind. It was only the sight of a string of frozen, multicolored long johns swinging stiffly in the breeze that showed someone was in residence.

We had come to this lonely place to meet Rowena Roye Rodgers, an independent type who, we had been told, had just sort of "arrived" about twenty-five years before and stayed. We figured anyone with the name Roye Rodgers had to be worth meeting, but we weren't sure of what we would find or if this person would be a suitable subject for a television feature story. We needn't have worried.

It was about twenty degrees below zero, and after banging

at the door in vain for five minutes, we were about to head back into the comparative warmth of the car. As a last resort, I tried the handle, and the door swung open on sagging hinges. It was as cold on the inside as it was on the out. There was no sign of life as we stepped into a kitchen that obviously hadn't been used for a long time. But now we could hear the sound of a radio playing behind a closed door to our left. Perhaps we were closing in on Rowena. We were becoming frozen to the core, and my knuckles were sore from beating on doors, but after a couple more minutes of pounding on the interior door, it opened. Not fully, just enough to reveal, about a foot lower than you would expect it, a grizzled face that barked, "Hang on a bit."

The door slammed shut, and all hell broke loose. There was no way we could imagine what was going on in that room. The language was turning the cold air blue, and it sounded as if a full-scale riot had broken out. An animal was screaming, and heavy thumping sounds were followed by the jangle of broken glass. Don and I exchanged worried glances. The unspoken question was, "Shall we just make a run for it and forget the whole thing?" Before we could make a decision, the door opened, fully this time, to reveal a tiny figure dressed in a woolen working shirt and a pair of baggy corduroy pants.

Rowena Roye Rodgers was seventy-four, not a whisker over five feet, and about ninety pounds. Not a large woman, but big enough, she explained, to corral a half-wild barn cat that had to be locked up before Don and I could enter the room. Otherwise, Rowena explained with salty embellishments, we would have been cat's meat.

The racket we had heard from the cold side of the door was her efforts to catch the creature and the mayhem that ensued when the cat crashed through the wire screen and became half crazed with fear when it got trapped between the screen and the window. Obviously even Rowena was terrified of the cat.

When we asked her what she had done with it, she waved at a door that led to the sleeping quarters above. The whole time we were in that house, we had on eye on that door.

Meet Roye Rodgers. "Nobody," she said, "ever calls me Rowena." This diminutive, scrappy woman lived through the long Minnesota winters in the one room in the house that had a source of heat. An old wood stove provided warmth and the ability to cook whatever food she and the cat needed. "It's all I need. Who the heck uses more than one room at a time anyway?" she asked. I asked her how she passed the time alone here off the beaten track with few friends and no relatives. "Read" was her one-word answer and, almost as an afterthought, "listen to classical music. I may not understand it, but I do know I like it."

"Let's go ouside and look around," I suggested, anxious to get on tape everything that made up the environment this remarkable woman had created for herself. "Fine," she said. "Want to see my sheep?"

Don had the camera rolling, and he backpedaled in front of Roye as she headed for the sheep pen. "I used to have running water here once," she said. "Some friends thought I should have it, but the dang thing froze up the first winter, and I haven't bothered with it since!"

She was proud of her little flock of sheep, but I wanted to talk about her. "Were you ever married, Roye?" "Yeah, twice. Walked out on them both." That, it seemed, was the end of that.

Back in the wood-stove warmth of her room, she offered a surprise invitation to visit her "cold storage." It turned out to be an adjoining room, an unheated, frigid depository of thousands of books — travel books, textbooks, books on art of all kinds, Greek philosophy, cookbooks, and novels. Roye had read or was reading them all. "Got most of 'em at library sales for a nickel apiece," she chortled happily. "Do you read everything?" I asked incredulously. "Sure. Trouble is, I don't understand half of what I read. But I do so want to know about all these things. Can you help me?"

It was a plea that went straight to my heart. Roye, living alone with just her books and a mad cat for company, was starved for intellectual conversation, for someone with whom she could discuss all the wonders she found unfolding from the pages of her fantastic library. As so often happens to reporters like us who pay such fleeting visits, we had to say, "Sorry, but we have to move on to our next story soon."

"Don't you have any friends?" I asked. "No, not what you would call close friends," she replied after some hesitation. "Maybe it's because I'm, I'm, I'm . . . " "A little too blunt?" I stuck in helpfully. "Yeah, that's it, too blunt!" she cried triumphantly.

THE RELUCTANT LADY
OF MCGARVEY SHOAL

WILLIAM LAMONT HARKNESS of Cleveland, Ohio, was one of the original investors in Standard Oil. Therefore, in the year 1911, he and his wife, Edith, had more money than they knew what to do with. So, what the heck, why not build a yacht, not just another floating status symbol, but a yacht that would be the finest to drop its anchor at the New York Yacht Club's fancy premises at Newport, Rhode Island.

The *Gunilda* was magnificent. Snow white from stem to stern, she weighed over six hundred tons before being loaded down with every conceivable luxury. Although driven by modern triple-expansion steam engines, *Gunilda* retained the racy look of a sailing yacht, with her two high masts and a bowsprit that leapt ahead of the hull for more than twenty feet. How fine she must have looked when Harkness loaded his family and friends on board in early August 1911 for a long cruise on the Great Lakes, with the sparkling sunshine reflecting off the deep, fresh water and the white of the hull and the tall funnel gleaming so you could see the ship for miles without the aid of binoculars. If you were lucky enough to be standing on the locks at Sault Ste. Marie, Michigan, as she came through that summer, you would have been struck by the sheer opulence of her. You may have noticed the small group of well-heeled passengers lounging around on the afterdeck, the men dressed rather inappropriately in suits and bowler hats, the women in long dresses, with parasols to shield their milky skins from the elements, and two white-coated stewards wheeling a trolley on the immaculately scrubbed decks — "Drinks all around, everyone?"

As the *Gunilda* rose the last few feet to the level of Lake Superior, the clanking mechanism slowly cranked the ponderous gates open to allow the yacht to enter the biggest of the Great Lakes. That's when you would have seen the stern of the yacht, the name *Gunilda* emblazoned in a curve that stretched across the entire width of the boat, in black to make it stand out against the white of the hull. But it was the gold that really would have caught your eye. Elaborate carvings in the oak and teak that had been lavishly used to complete the hull were covered with a solid coat of gold leaf. White and gold, what a beautiful command Captain Alex Korkum had that day.

As *Gunilda* cleared the mouth of St. Marys River, Captain Korkum went into a mahogany paneled room behind the wheelhouse. From a solid oak chest of drawers, he selected a chart that covered the northeastern portion of Lake Superior, leaned over it thoughtfully, and began to chart a course for the farthest north you can go in the Great Lakes, Nipigon Bay in Ontario, Canada.

The reason owner Bill Harkness wanted to take his yacht to such a remote but beautiful spot has not survived the years, but the passengers on board were not dependent on where they were or where they were going. There was plenty of fine food to eat and a cellar of the finest wines. As the sun set in a hazy fire of red and yellows over the vast expanse of Superior, they gathered around the grand piano in the saloon, raised their crystal glasses, and sang romantic songs to each other.

It took several days to cover the two hundred miles across the lake, and Captain Korkum had to be sure that when he did approach the Canadian coast it was during daylight hours. There were no lighthouses or beacons to show him the way, and the entrance to Nipigon Bay was narrow and dotted with islands. This was Korkum's first visit to this remote place, and he asked Harkness for permission to hire a local pilot. Harkness, multimillionaire, philanthropist, owner of the most luxurious yacht afloat, spendthrift, and stockholder, refused to cough up twenty-five dollars to have his yacht guided safely to its destination of Rossport in Nipigon Bay. So Korkum himself turned the prow of *Gunilda* into the riverlike waterways that threaded between the islands of the bay.

It looked clear. A straight run between two pine-covered islands, fine weather, and nothing in sight. *Gunilda* was given her head, and she cut through the water with her destroyerlike bow. The engines pounded dully below, barely vibrating the silverware on the Irish linen tablecloths as the holidaymakers sat down for lunch.

The grinding noise came first, an irritating sound like fingernails on a chalkboard. Then the movement, or rather the arresting of movement. Knives slid silently across the tablecloth and fetched up against the crystal water glasses, which rang like bells. Then, from the galley, came the sickening crash of priceless china. Next came the violent lurch that brought everyone off their chairs onto the floor in a tangled heap of bodies, crockery, trays, drinks, and untasted food.

On the bridge, Captain Korkum looked incredulously over the bow. Where a few seconds before he had been looking at a horizon of virgin forest was now clear blue with a smatter-

83

ıng of wind-torn clouds. His ship was pointing up instead of at. Looking over the side of the ship, Korkum immediately saw the reason for the unscheduled stop. Just below the surface, grey against the dark green of the surrounding water, were shards of rock that marked the top of an underwater mountain called McGarvey Shoal.

You couldn't blame Captain Korkum. No marker showed the hazard; only locals, like the fisherman Harvey McGarvey, who was the first to wreck his boat on the shoal, knew it was there. And, of course, the pilot knew, the pilot who wanted twenty-five dollars to guide the *Gunilda* safely into Rossport.

Not a man to waste time bemoaning his fate, Harkness swiftly organized a fleet of fishing boats from nearby Rossport to evacuate his passengers and crew in time for lunch ashore. Calls went out to Port Arthur, just sixty miles away, for a tug, and one was smartly dispatched. Harkness was confident the Scottish shipbuilders who had constructed the *Gunilda* had done a fine job. She was not taking water, and so much of the hull was high and dry it was obvious the damage was confined to scratches in the steel of her bottom.

Twenty-four hours after she ran aground on McGarvey Shoal, *Gunilda* was ready to be refloated. The ship remained exactly as she had been the minute she hit the rocks. Everyone was ashore drinking merrily in the Rossport Inn as the tug took the strain on its six-inch Manila ropes. With the same grinding noise she made when she went on, *Gunilda* lurched slowly backwards off the underwater mountain top.

The tug captain watched with satisfaction as he met his contract, but his smile froze when he noticed the open portholes at *Gunilda*'s stern. He suddenly realized that as the ship slid off the rock, her stern was dipping below the waterline. It was too late. The yacht was now sliding of her own weight, and the water reached ports farther along the hull. They too were open to the icy waters of Lake Superior, and the process speeded up. Yelling wildly, the crew of the tug grabbed axes and started to chop at the straining ropes. One by one they parted with a snap, barely preventing their own little craft from being dragged under by the sinking yacht.

With a sigh and a gurgle, the world's finest and newest luxury yacht disappeared, virtually undamaged, beneath the waves. She sank slowly, dispelling the air trapped in all the interior spaces in a cloud of bubbles that covered half an acre, until she settled, right side up, three hundred feet below. And that was almost the end of the story of the *Gunilda*.

Nearly seventy years later, in my never-ending search for television stories that are unusual and extraordinary, I saw a newspaper clipping that described a Canadian man's quest to salvage a unique wreck. His name was Fred Broennle, and cameraman Bill Juntenen and I met him in 1980.

We had never heard of the yacht *Gunilda*, but Fred had. In fact, years before, he had, he claimed, gained all rights to the wreck from the insurers Lloyds of London.

We met Fred in a clapboard building on a dock in Thunder Bay, Ontario. The sign on the door said in blue and white paint:

Deep Diving Systems Ltd.
MARINE CONTRACTORS

Fred sat behind a desk that looked out over the harbor. He wore a brown, military-type shirt with epaulets. The sleeves were rolled up over brawny arms, and a big, fat wristwatch, like a diver's watch, adorned his left wrist. He looked to be about forty years old, a square-looking man with a broad face topped with a mop of dark, curly hair. Fred was of German extraction, and his voice still retained a trace of accent.

"Every wreck has a mystery about it, and the *Gunilda* definitely does," he said. "Rumors have been going around that there is three million dollars worth of jewelry on board, but I rather believe that, knowing women, women would go to a lot of trouble to get their jewelry. They might even risk their lives."

Fred was well-known around the city of Thunder Bay, as much for his failures as for his successes. But he was perhaps best recognized as the man who had a fixation on the seventy-year-old wreck that lay beneath the frigid waters of Lake Superior in Nipigon Bay, just sixty miles to the northwest.

Fred was telling us his theories about what, if anything, was left aboard the ship. "The *Gunilda* ran aground and sat there for a day before she was pulled free. I'm sure the women got their jewelry off. However, when you talk about riches, there are artifacts. Every porthole, every instrument is, as far as I'm concerned, equivalent to a diamond or gold bullion. The triple-expansion engines in there, the scrollwork, the whole ship itself is, as far as I'm concerned, a jewelry store."

But, Fred said, it wasn't the riches of the ship that made the *Gunilda* such a passion in his life. Part of the fascination stemmed from one fateful August day in 1970, when his best friend, King Haig, died while diving on the wreck. For ten long years, Fred had lived with the knowledge that he and King had broken a cardinal rule of diving: Never dive alone!

"I felt somewhat responsible for letting him dive by himself even though it was beyond my control to stop him." Our interview had suddenly taken on a somber tone. We had not known of this tragedy when we sat down. It was a stunning turn to the story, and there were more surprises to come. Fred continued ruminating. "The day King went down, I was in a bathing suit and he was suited up. He wasn't supposed to go down. He was supposed to go just a few feet under the water, eighty feet, and he decided to go all the way." It was too long ago for tears, but obviously the loss of his friend while diving on the wreck of the *Gunilda* had had a profound effect on this tough marine salvager.

From that day, what had been just a hobby turned into an obsession and a business for Fred Broennle. At one point, he persuaded a group of investors to fund the building of a remote-controlled submersible, ostensibly to aid in general salvage work but in Fred's mind suited for one task only—the raising of the *Gunilda*. It was a marvel of underwater engineering and cost a million and a half dollars. But Fred never used it before he was forced to sell it to satisfy creditors.

Undeterred from his ambition, Fred went to Europe and bought special underwater TV cameras from Lubeck and Keil in Germany, and as soon as the weather permitted, he and a large crew of helpers lowered the cameras for a first look in seventy years at the wreck of the yacht *Gunilda*. The tapes of that historic occasion still exist, gathering dust in cardboard boxes stacked in Fred's waterside office. As we viewed highlights from the black-and-white tapes, Fred described what happened as they maneuvered the camera around the stricken ship. "I was in the control room above, and the camera got caught up on the stays on the port side of *Gunilda*. We had to drop the camera down in order to get away from the wires so we could then bring it back up in the clear. As we scanned the bottom, we saw King's body. He was lying right by the ship, about six feet from the hull."

On the tape, the camera swung slowly around, and there, on the bottom, we could see a left leg with a flipper on the foot. Another angle showed the whole man lying on his back, tilted slightly by the two large air tanks still strapped securely to his back. We could hear the gasps of horror in the control room and Fred's voice clearly saying, "That's King! There's King!"

Fred was still talking about that dramatic day six years before. "The whole crew knew we were going to find him sooner or later. We somewhat expected to find him in the ship rather than outside." The crew overcame the shock of their macabre discovery and brought the body to the surface with a grappling hook. Fred gave us a vivid lesson in the preserving powers of three hundred feet of icy Lake Superior waters. "As far as condition goes, you might as well say you deep-freeze him. There was absolutely no decomposition taking place. There was a little skin missing around his mouth, and that was it!"

As a result of our research into this dramatic story, we found a couple of young scuba divers in Duluth, Minnesota, who had successfully dived down to the *Gunilda* with color movie cameras and lights. Jerry Buchanan and Bob Horton were more than happy to make their footage available to us for inclusion in our story, and we, for the first time, got a good look at what Fred had sought for so long.

It was indeed a spectacular sight, unmarked except where vandalistic opportunists had dragged anchors across her hull in the hopes of snagging something of value, creating smashed bulwarks, breaking a mast, and laying the long, white funnel flat on the deck.

Just as Fred had said, everything was still there. The underwater cameras showed the filigree in gold that graced the bow and stern. Brass lamps still hung in their brackets, and oak skylight covers were still in place. Snakelike coils of rope still wound around the cast-iron bitts, cut off short by the hasty axes of the tug crew. The diver shone his light into the chart room where Captain Korkum had plotted his fateful course seventy years before. The charts were gone, but the oak and mahogany cabinets still held their secrets, and they were still locked! On the wall was a magnificent brass nautical clock, a collector's item worth a fortune. On the bow, the bell was still hanging near a flagstaff that had been bent double by a marauding thief working safely and illegally from the surface.

Jerry watched his film with us and described the feeling of swimming freely among so much untouched history. "We got to the point where nitrogen narcosis was manageable, and we could function down there. We realized that it's a treasure ship as far as Great Lakes wrecks go. Everything that's there is like an antique. In one of the rooms, we saw a gold-and-crystal chandelier leaning against a grand piano. There's silver dishes just sitting there for the taking, almost, if it weren't for the depths."

On the film, one of the divers swims up to a door, but it was locked. Strange that a door should be locked and the portholes left open. The other way around, and *Gunilda* would have floated free, and none of us would have heard of her.

Bob took up the story as the film unfolded. "It's beautiful. When you get to know the *Gunilda*, you fall in love with her. She's just gorgeous, and I don't know if I could take anything off the ship. It's really neat. There's all that fantastic junk that's broken off and laying on the deck. It isn't junk! It's high-class stuff that's just been misplaced."

We watched the puffs of fine silt billow away from the diver's hand as he swept it like dust off a brass binnacle that still carried a working compass. "There's all kinds of things that you could never even dream about finding on a shipwreck, and they are just sitting there, untouched." Now we realized the diver we had been watching on the film was indeed Bob, and he was reliving the magic moments he had spent on the decks of *Gunilda*, three hundred feet below the waves of Lake Superior.

"I was the first person to swim to the stern steering wheel and just stand behind it," he said. We watched the shadowy figure in a blue dry suit drift eerily across the stern of the ship and up to the wheel. The compass-holding binnacle gleamed in the powerful filming lights. Jerry continued describing how it felt. "It was a really neat feeling. It was like being the skipper of the vessel."

To complete our story of the Reluctant Lady of McGarvey Shoal and her lover, Fred Broennle, we chartered a boat and one sunny fall day motored out onto Nipigon Bay with Fred and a bottle of rum. Fred enjoyed several tots from the bottle as we sped across the unruffled waters of this picturesque corner of Lake Superior. By the time he cut the engine and we drifted slowly over McGarvey Shoal, Fred was a little maudlin.

Leaning over the bow and staring into the inky black depths, Fred said, "I'd really like to get going on the salvage. It's been quite a few years now since I started this project, and it's always money and time, and the contracts I have to finish. And first thing you know, it's winter and the storms are here." I noticed that Fred's German accent had become a little more obvious. Was it the rum? Or was it because he was affected by the proximity of his obsession? "Right here, that's where she dry-docked herself," said Fred, pointing at the rock-covered mountaintop clearly visible just a few feet below the surface. "And this is as close as I can get to her." "Would you like to get a little closer, Fred?" I asked in a deliberate attempt to get him to tell us how he really felt.

"Well, eventually she's got to come up. I've been woking towards zees for ten years now," he said wistfully. I wasn't satisfied that Fred had opened up to us completely, and I tried to unlock his heart with another question. "How do you feel, sitting so close to something that has consumed your life for ten years? It's so near and yet so far."

"Well, Jason, it's hard to explain. Let's just put it this way. This is where it all started ten years ago, and I hope it doesn't end here, but eventually I'll bring her up. I've had a lot of disappointments. However, we are getting closer. We have the

90

technology now, how to work deep in cold water. We know about the core temperature of the diver. We know how a man working underwater has to decompress. I think we've mastered all that, so now it's just a rigging job. However," he shrugged resignedly, "money is an important point here. I've put a lot of money into this, and before she's up, there's going to be a lot more money spent."

Fred gunned the engine of the motor cruiser to put us back on top of McGarvey Shoal, which we had drifted from in the light winds. "What I'm trying to accomplish is to raise six hundred tons from three hundred feet in the coldest water known to divers. And this is just the start. There are two thousand known wrecks in the Great Lakes, and it is an exciting thought to be able to see just one-tenth of what's at the bottom of the lakes. There is an estimated sixteen thousand wrecks altogether in the Great Lakes, so every time a diver goes down, he's just liable to run into a wreck." Fred's eyes were bright with excitement at the thought of salvaging the riches rusting away underwater. But his story was the story of the *Gunilda*, not the thousands of other sunken ships littering the lake bed.

One last question, the most important question, the question we set out to settle at the beginning of our quest. "Why, Fred? Why this compulsion to raise the *Gunilda*?"

"Well, Jason, I feel the *Gunilda* owes me something. I lost a buddy on it nine years ago. And yet, I feel I owe the *Gunilda* something too. She's a beautiful wreck. I don't even want to call her a wreck. She's just sitting down there waiting to be lifted. It changed my life. I might as well live on a different planet. I lost my first wife; she just couldn't hack this type of a venture. I've started a new business, successfully. I've built a submersible, all with the thought in mind that eventually it's going to work and I can bring up the *Gunilda*.

"Some people call me a poor businessman. I don't know, maybe I am. But I put a lot of money into what we are sitting right over right now, and one day she's going to come up or else I stay down. That's the way I feel about it. I think that sums it up."

Ten years sweep by. On the eve of publishing this book in 1989, Fred answers the phone at his home in Thunder Bay. He sounds just the same, with his distinctive German accent, but tired. He is very happy to hear from me, full of news about a documentary maker that had come by with plans to make another film about the *Gunilda*. Yes, the ship still lay, virtually untouched, beneath the icy waters of Nipigon Bay, with the innkeeper at the Rossport Hotel keeping an eye on suspicious boats hovering near her. A phone call to Fred would result in them being chased away, not by Fred but by the Royal Canadian Mounted Police (waterborne division, presumably). "Absolutely," says Fred. "I am listed as the legal owner by Lloyds of London. No one can touch anything on that wreck but me." And in answer to my question, Fred confirms he still burns with the fever that will not be cooled until the *Gunilda* floats again or, as he says, he stays down. But he is running out of steam. Always a man on the edge, Fred has had a series of bad business breaks in the intervening years. He says he's still in marine salvage but has no money to finance a serious effort to realize his life's dream. But he is not without hope or plans.

"I had to move the tank from Rossport because the locals began to complain." "What tank?" I asked, perplexed at this sudden change of subject to an area that seemed to have no bearing on what we were talking about. "The storage tank," replied Fred in his fractured accent. He was beginning to warm to the subject, whatever it was, and his speech became more difficult to understand as his excitement grew and the words came faster. "Seveny fit wide an fordy fit high. Too beeg, and de say I add to tow it away." It was a ninety-ton oil storage tank that Fred had somehow got as far as Rossport.

The week I spoke to him, he had been forced to tow the rusting monstrosity out of sight of the visitors and residents around pretty Rossport. It was, as we spoke, bobbing ponderously in a cove not far from McGarvey Shoal.

Fred, it turned out, had another plan. It was to place the huge tank over the *Gunilda*, fill it with water until it sank, attach it to straps placed around the sunken hull three hundred feet below, pump out the water, and bingo, the yacht would free herself of the sticky grasp of the bottom silt and be easily towed into the shallows.

So after all the years of sacrifice and cost, Fred Broennle is no closer to the Reluctant Lady of McGarvey Shoal than he ever was. But in all those years, he was never without a plan. I suspect that if I call him back in another ten years, he will still perk up at the mention of his dream and in his deep voice with its European base, tell of his latest exciting scheme to raise the *Gunilda*.

KIDS WHO EAT
FLOWERS

IT WAS AN unusual problem. A live animal had to be transferred from a zoo in Texas to a zoo in St. Paul, Minnesota. But this animal was a baby too young to survive the trauma of being packed in a case and shipped by air, and no airline was ready to admit the youngster into the passenger cabin of its aircraft.

Continuing a long history of support for Como Zoo in St. Paul, Stanley S. Hubbard, owner of KSTP and my employer, offered to make his corporate aircraft available to bring the animal to Minnesota. It was a natural story for "On the Road Again," so cameraman Ben Threinen and I hopped on the plane for the long flight to Brownsville, Texas. For company on the flight we had Arlene and Joe Scheunemann. It was this couple who were going to pick up their new baby. As we were to find out, this was not the first time that Arlene had volunteered to be foster mother to an abandoned wild thing.

It's a beautiful facility, the Brownsville Zoo. The balmy Gulf of Mexico weather makes it a popular year-round place of entertainment and education for residents and visitors alike. The exhibits are large and open to the sky, surrounded by a background of luxuriant green plants and palm trees, gigantic outdoor versions of the expensive indoor varieties we are familiar with in northern states like Minnesota. There is a distinct Mexican flavor to this zoo. The entry is reminiscent of the facade of an old mission, complete with bells.

In bright sunshine, Arlene and Joe strolled along the wide boulevards between signs that indicated the homes of tropical birds, African gazelle, and alligators. They were headed for the great apes enclosure and, Arlene hoped, an emotional reunion with an old friend.

"Tamu, Tamu," Arlene called across the crystal clear moat that separated the public from some of their closest relatives in the animal world. The lumbering gorilla named Tamu ignored the pleading call of her former human foster mother. Tamu was eleven years old now, but when she was a baby, she was abandoned by her mother and raised for her first year by Arlene Scheunemann. She is one of the few people in the world who is prepared to take these orphans of the ape kingdom into her home and raise them as if they were her own children. Not that she hasn't had her own share of human children. Joe and Arlene have a grown family of two girls and two boys.

But unlike human babies, gorillas when they grow up apparently don't feel any residual fondness for their parents, natural animal or foster human.

Tamu, then, was of the past, but Arlene was here for the future of Tamu's son. Just a few weeks old, this tiny jet-black offspring of Tamu and her partner, Lamidoc, was in desperate need of a mother who would care for him with love and affection, something that his bumptious mother was not interested in doing.

As yet without a name, the little ape frolicked with a blanket in a tidy animal nursery at the Brownsville Zoo. Just a few weeks old, he weighed a little more than eight pounds. He looked curiously at the little clutch of humans staring down at him. His black eyes appeared to take up a third of his face, a face that seemed to be covered in shiny black leather. His inky black hair stood up like a crew cut on his head but also continued all over his body. Long arms gathered the blanket around his body as if it provided security. There must be something in all of us that responds to babies, animal or human, because this little fella was irresistible.

Seeing the baby gorilla in these circumstances made it easier to understand why this handsome, middle-aged woman from St. Paul would elect to take what is, after all, a wild animal into her home. Arlene and Joe would hand raise him for about a year until he was old enough and big enough to fend for himself at Como Zoo in St. Paul, where he would spend the rest of his life.

We had our camera set up, with the entrance to the Brownsville Zoo in the background. A zoo employee, a woman smartly dressed in a khaki uniform, came out of a long, low building that held the animal nursery. In her arms was a little bundle of joy that now had a name, "Casey," dubbed as the result of a joint decision by Arlene and Joe, who are experienced in such things.

"Oh, my goodness, aren't you just a doll," said a very excited Arlene as the furry, black infant was placed in her arms. Casey seemed happy enough, with his left thumb stuck firmly in his mouth and his right hand clutching his security blanket. Joe got to carry the diapers.

The ride home in Stanley Hubbard's corporate aircraft was

97

uneventful. Casey slept soundly, except for the time he spent sucking noisily on several bottles of milk that Arlene had thoughtfully brought along.

The next time we saw Casey, it was Christmas. He was six months old and quite a handful. Not only that, but he had a sister of sorts—a seven-and-a-half-month-old orangoutang named Katie.

The front room of Arlene and Joe's home, on a quiet residential street not far from St. Paul's Como Zoo, was very festive. A large tree covered in stars, tinsel, and lights took up an entire corner. Gifts were piled beneath the tree, with wrappings of many colors that made the presents part of the decorations. Garlands and paper bells and angels hung from the walls, and a baby gorilla and baby orangoutang hung from climbing bars in the center of the room.

It was a difficult scene to take in with one glance. The two little figures were dressed in nice new holiday clothes, Katie in a bright red dress trimmed with lots of snow white lace and Casey with a blue and white knit shirt and red pants with suspenders to match. He as black. She was brown. Otherwise, they looked like brother and sister playing happily with one another on the rug. But as soon as Arlene stepped into the room, Katie scuttled across and leapt into her arms. The needs of these little apes may be the same as human babies, but they have a big advantage. When Katie and Casey want something, they just go get it.

"They have to be hugged. They need all this holding and attention, just like a human baby." Arlene peered over the furry head of Katie, who had wrapped herself tightly around Arlene's upper body in a hold that looked like it was forever. "The only way you can provide this kind of attention to them is to let them right into the family," she said.

Another six months went by before we saw the two special

youngsters again. It was summer, and Arlene was trying to do some gardening. Trouble was, a rambunctious Casey was eating the flowers, and Katie was getting tangled in her favorite plaything, an aluminum garden lounger. They had grown alarmingly. Although they were about a year old, they were approaching a size and strength that meant it was no longer practical for them to stay in a private home. It was getting embarrassing for the Scheunemanns, too. The apes insisted on going with them when they went for outings in the family car.

"People in other cars will often do a double take and chuckle, probably thinking they are seeing things." Arlene said, "Or sometimes they will quickly look away, obviously thinking what ugly children we have."

For more than a year, while Arlene was acting as foster mother to Casey and Katie, the authorities at Como Zoo had been building a new home for the apes. And inevitably, the day came when they had to make the move.

It was a large spacious area, complete with rubber tires, balls, and other toys for the young gorilla and orangoutang to play with. The front wall was constructed entirely of glass, giving everyone there that day a good view of the drama that was about to unfold. Arlene, with two furry beings attached to her like limpets, walked into the enclosure and peeled the sinewy arms from her body. It took a while, but finally she managed to step away and quickly jump through a door at the back. Casey went crazy. Separated from the only mother he had ever known for the first time, he screamed blue murder. His mouth spread wide open, showing every tooth he had as he screeched his unhappiness for the world to hear.

Arlene stood rooted to the spot. The door closed behind her but didn't shut out the noise of the brokenhearted gorilla. Tears welled in her eyes as she stepped away, carefully avoiding the glass panel at the front. It had to be a quick break, and in her heart she knew, just as Tamu had not recognized her in Brownsville, this little animal would also soon forget.

Casey the gorilla is now a favorite among visitors to Como Zoo in St. Paul. It's hoped he will one day father his own children and help perpetuate the endangered species to which he belongs. But most of all, everyone, especially Arlene Scheunemann, hopes that the mother of Casey's child will take care of her own babies.

A DOCTOR FOR EL CASCO

IT WAS A fascinating story, a Minnesota man spending all his vacation time in a remote village in Mexico caring for the sick. I gained approval for cameraman Ben Threinen and me to travel to Mexico to produce a series of stories on the subject, and we made our plans.

A couple of calls to the Mexican Consulate in St. Paul and everything seemed to be in order. We were to enter Mexico through Mazatlan and then travel internally by air to Durango, where we would pick up a car to drive to the little village of El Casco in the Sierra Madres.

We made one big mistake. A slight change in our travel plans meant that we would arrive in Guadalajara and not Mazatlan. Our error became evident when, with a great sense of excitement and anticipation, we stepped off the plane at Guadalajara Airport.

It's always a tense moment for us, trying to get our equipment through customs wherever we travel. Our cameras,

101

recorders, microphones, and other complicated electronic equipment costs tens of thousands of dollars and is viewed with great suspicion by the officials who guard the portals of foreign countries. But we are careful to carry the appropriate documents and to make sure we are welcome. So it was with a wary confidence that we approached the customs counter at Guadalajara.

We hauled our mountain of crates and packages up to the inspector and tried to look competely unconcerned as he stared at us. Ben handed over the documentation we had carried from the Mexican Consulate in St. Paul, and nothing happened. The usual bang of the rubber stamp was held in abeyance, and a torrent of Spanish issued forth, which neither of us understood. I began to get the feeling we were in trouble. I mentally computed our travel plans. We were scheduled out of Guadalajara the next day to Durango, and we were meeting our story subject in the mountains the next day. We could not afford a delay; there was no way to contact the people we were to meet. They were only planning on spending a couple of days in the village. We had to get our gear through customs now!

To our amazement and distress, and without any understanding of the problem on our part, three burly Mexican officials loaded all of our equipment onto a trolley, hauled it across the customs hall, and promptly locked it in a cage with a huge, old-fashioned padlock.

"You will get your things back later, when the chief of customs comes back." The words we understood, what we didn't comprehend was that the statement was a lie.

Next morning, bright and early, Ben and I were at the chief of customs' office. We knew we were in the right place because there was only one parking space in the shade. It was his. It was nine o'clock, and we waited there until three in the afternoon. We were continually assured that Senor Vargas, the customs chief, would be here any minute. They lied. They lied through their teeth. They lied looking us straight in the eyes.

The problem was that we really didn't know what the problem was. In retrospect, we know that the matching documents to those that we carried had gone to our original destination of Mazatlan. We were in Guadalajara. Ergo, we were stuck.

To cut a long and frustrating story short, it took us four days to persuade the customs officials that we were legitimate news gatherers and we had a perfect right to enter the country with our equipment. Four days! When we finally left for Durango, we had no idea if the story we had come to cover was still happening.

The van we rented in Durango to make the hundred-mile drive into the Sierra Madres was a wreck. It was old, and the doors were ill-fitting. Dust poured through and covered us and everything we carried with us. It was hot, and we were miserable not knowing what lay ahead. Finally, a road sign said:

This was Pancho Villa country, with hills rather than mountains rolling off into the hazy blue distance, covered with a brown carpet of dessicated grass and punctuated with stunted trees and shrubs. A desert for most of the year, a swamp when the rains came in July.

103

El Casco was only a hundred yards off the highway, with one main street of low adobe buildings baking harder each day in the searing heat. It was the middle of the day, and the only sign of life was a clutch of chickens scratching a meager living around the steps of the houses.

But one building was different. It was made of unfinished concrete blocks and stood on its own lot in the center of town. It was, as we knew from our directions, the clinic that had been created by the drive and dedication of one man, a forty-year-old office worker from Bloomington, Minnesota, named Roger Belisle. My heart was in my mouth as we climbed stiffly and gratefully from the rickety van and walked up the three steps to the door. There was no sign that anyone was there, and we feared that our four-day delay had made us too late.

"Hi, glad you guys made it." A big man, balding on top, with dark hair laid down neatly on each side of his head, carrying a little too much weight around his middle, dressed in a western-style, short-sleeved shirt and jeans, came to the door before we even had a chance to knock.

"I'm Roger Belisle, and this is my wife, Eva." Roger gestured to a woman by his side who was dwarfed by his bulk. Eva, with her long black hair and dark, flashing eyes, was obviously Mexican and, it turned out, was the reason this unusual family came to this remote village several times each year.

"Eva was born here, you know," Roger said. "Her father was the victim of a political assassination a few years ago. Come on, I'll introduce you to the man who exacted revenge for her."

We walked as a group down the dusty main street of El Casco, which was still deserted because of the midday heat. Up on a hill, a man appeared on a white horse who, at a wave from Roger, spurred himself and his mount forward and downward toward us at a full gallop. "This is the local sheriff," Roger said as the horseman wheeled up to us in a flurry of dust. "He killed one of my father-in-law's assassins in a gunfight." The sheriff stared at us strangers from under his ten-gallon straw hat. The stub of a small cigar stuck impudently from the center of his tightly compressed lips. His dark face scowled at the two gringos, especially at Ben, who was gamely pointing his video camera at him.

But we were not intimidated. After all, we had just spent four days trying to get our gear back from the most dangerous of all Mexicans—bureaucrats!

"He saw him up on a hill." Roger continued with his story of the great El Casco shoot-out. "He was far away. The sheriff was on his horse, and the other guy was on his. They looked at each other, and the sheriff saw a puff of white smoke. He dropped off his horse, rolled on the ground, and got off two shots with his rifle. The other man dropped. He had made his last political assassination."

This, then, was the environment that Roger's wife had grown up in, and the tales she told her husband while sitting in their comfortable home in Bloomington stirred his imagination. Roger was particularly moved by his wife's description of the squalid and unhealthy conditions the villagers of her hometown had to bear. When she told him that the nearest clinic was more than a hundred miles from El Casco and even if the villagers could make the journey they couldn't afford the doctor's fees, Roger had to see for himself.

"We came here so my wife could show me where she was born, and I saw the people were really sick. Many of them were dying. Some babies perished while we were here, and I learned that some people died just from a very high temperature because they didn't have aspirin."

Roger was no doctor, at least not qualified to practice medicine in Minnesota or any other state in the United States. But the plight of the peasants of his wife's birthplace moved him deeply. There must be someting he could do. He continued. "At that point I said, 'Well, I can provide aspirin.' And that was the start of everything."

So for the first time in the two-hundred-year history of this small Mexican village, someone cared enough to provide fundamental health care. His name was Roger Belisle, and they called him "Doctor."

There was no questioning the people of El Casco's need for medical help. Their adobe homes had no sanitation beyond a bucket that they either dumped in the gutter outside or, if they felt up to it, threw into a river along the southern edge of town that was reduced by drought to a trickle. We watched the kids prepare for the school day by doing group exercises in the playground. They were clean and reasonably well dressed, but their pinched faces showed the lack of nutrition that haunted their lives and made them weak and subject to infection.

On the north side of town, the cemetery, surrounded by a handlaid stone wall, had two parts. It was almost equally divided between the ground for grown-ups and the last resting place for innumerable children. I walked between these tiny graves, each one well tended, each with its own large cement cross, recording a commentary that we would later weave into the story of El Casco and its strange "doctor" from the North. "They say in El Casco that if you make it past the age of two, you have a chance at life," I said with genuine feeling aroused by the sight of so many little graves, some surrounded by adobe steps painted light blue with sprays of plastic flowers in colorful pots. I continued, "But many don't make it, and that is why half the cemetery here is reserved for babies."

Our scene now shifts to the inside of the only concrete building in town, the clinic that has been under construction by Roger and his family for nearly ten years.

106

The inside walls are exactly like the outside, rough cement, but it is cooler here, and Roger looks confidently efficient in his short white coat with a stethoscope around his neck. Behind him is a rack built of one-by-two pine furring strips purchased at Knox Lumber and hauled two-thousand miles south. An impressive display of drugs fills the shelves. Closer inspection shows they are all older than the dates of expiration stamped on their labels. Roger explains that the drugs are all donated by clinics and hospitals in Minnesota. They are still potent and will help alleviate the suffering of the people in El Casco no matter what the date on the label says.

A young boy, about eight years old, is the first patient that "Doctor" Belisle sees while Eva calms the dozen or so that are packed, sweltering, in an adjoining room. In fluent Spanish, the "doctor" talks down to the beaming upturned face of the child, and he prescribes the only thing he can for the obvious malnutrition—vitamins. I get the feeling that Roger's large, clean, cool hand laid on the boys hair is going to be a tonic that will do the lad good with or without drugs.

"Just by being here, we have given the people hope." Roger was talking to us as Eva ushered a pregnant woman through the curtain that covered the concrete opening, lacking a door, that separated the two rooms of the clinic. "They know we are going to do everything we can to help them. And it's true. We will. We will do whatever we can. When people have nothing, how can you refuse to help them?" The patient is very pregnant, and she has a child under two on her lap. Roger examines the mother and child, two for the price of one. The cost to her? Nothing. Gesturing toward the little expanding family, Roger says, "I can't look at them and say it's hopeless and then return to my nice home in Minnesota, sit in front of my television set, and relax, knowing that these people are suffering so."

On the outside, El Casco is like a thousand other Mexican villages. In the heat of the day, a mangy dog snaps at the flies with what little spunk it has left. A pig noses under a stoop, raising little dust devils with each snort of its nostrils. A tired-looking man comes down the street, crunched under the weight of two buckets of water hanging from a bridle across his shoulders. Two children, a girl aged about six in a bright red dress dragging a little boy about two whose pants cover his bare feet, wander towards the river to help their mother, who has been bending over the trickle of murky water washing clothes for several hours. El Casco is like a thousand other Mexican villages, but for the cement clinic in the center of town and the self-styled "doctor" who comes a couple of times a year to save a life or two, a one-man, nonprofit organization: The American-Mexican Medical Foundation.

We ended our tale of El Casco and its good fortune with a final comment from Roger as we stood on the gravelly, dry river bed looking up at the village. "A lot of times I think it would be wonderful if I could help everyone. You know, everyone in Mexico, in all of the world. But I'm only one person, so I'll try to enlist the help of other people. Then more will be done. In the meantime," he said, "I cannot turn my back on them."

A DOG YOU CAN
COUNT ON

IT WAS A perfectly natural scene. A middle-aged man walking his dog on a snow-covered street in the Iron Range town of Aurora in northern Minnesota. Bill Ojala didn't work any longer, but he had led a full and exciting life as an attorney and Minnesota state legislator. His ten-year-old miniature collie, Sadie, had led a useful and satisfying life too and was, like her master, enjoying the fruits of retirement.

Bill was dressed in a light brown parka, without gloves, so his hands were out of sight, withdrawn into the long sleeves of his coat. He had not lost his hair; indeed, it was fashionably long, streaked with grey, and fell over his forehead. I guessed he was in his late fifties, still with a bounce in his stride as he led his dog, who obediently trotted at his side at the end of a long, slender chain.

It was our first meeting with this unusual couple. A pair, Bill claimed, that had established a rapport so strong they could communicate without speech, or barking. In fact, a story I'd seen in a local Iron Range paper said Sadie could do simple arithmetic.

Good enough for me. Bill Ojala was happy to have us set up our camera in the neat living room of the unassuming house he and his wife lived in in Aurora, and he was delighted to show off the unusual talents of his best buddy, Sadie.

We were ready to document Sadie's abilities. Bill sat on the edge of an oak kitchen chair, leaning forward with his arms on his knees, his heels raised, intently looking at his dog. In his left hand, he held a fragment of her favorite biscuit treat.

Sadie sat with both front legs held out in front of her, the left leg a little higher and straighter than the right, her tail acting as a balance. It was a strange pose, rather like a kangaroo. Her eyes never left her master's, and her shiny black nose never twitched. Her light brown eyebrows were arched in a way that gave her a look of perpetual surprise. Bill and Sadie in the center of the room formed a strange tableau.

There were a few seconds of perfect silence, but neither of them flinched when Bill suddenly spoke. "What's seven plus two take away six? Seven plus two take away six?" Just a beat of time for the dog to think about it, and Bill held out his right hand, palm upwards. Sadie reached up with her left front paw and gently but firmly stroked Bill's palm—once, twice, three times, and then, positively, she stopped. There was no apparent move from Bill during this performance, no hint of even a wink. "That's right," said Bill, and he offered the tiny treat, which was taken with a grateful snap.

They repeated the scene. "What's three times three?" Sadie knew that one. Nine strokes across her master's palm resulted in another piece of biscuit. "Smart dog," he said as she maintained her pose, waiting for more problems to solve.

This dog, Bill claimed, was so smart she could even do square roots. We were really skeptical about this claim, despite evidence that Sadie had a pretty good grasp of figures. "What's

110

the square root of nine? What number multiplied by itself equals nine?" Bill asked Sadie, who had not moved from her original pose. The camera moved in for a close-up of the dog as she confidently hit Bill's palm again — the correct three times.

Okay, so the dog could do basic math, but what about Bill's claim that there was some kind of extrasensory perception between him and his pet?

To test this allegation, I placed myself beside the dog so the camera could record my actions but the dog could not see what I was doing. I raised my left hand to the camera with four fingers outstretched. Bill then issued his instructions. "Okay, Sadie, Jason is thinking of a number between one and ten. Put yourself in his head and tell us what he is thinking about. Got that?" Bill took the right number on his hand and grinning triumphantly said, "Four! Was that right? Guess so."

Not content with astounding us with his pet's ability to work out problems in English, Bill then tried to convince us that as the result of a recent visit to their home by a Finnish exchange student, Sadie could also count and do arithmetic in Finnish. Having no understanding of that Scandanavian language, we couldn't vouch for the accuracy of the next demonstration, but Bill and Sadie looked pleased at its conclusion.

Bill was unshakable in his belief that Sadie could count. Pointing at his own temple, he said, "I think it's some kind of mental communication. There is no trick, no trick."

We'll never know if Sadie and Bill pulled a fast one on us that day. Reviewing the videotape, there is no evidence of any communication between the two that would have explained what happened. It doesn't matter. Both of them were obviously very happy at the attention we gave them in their retirement, and we came away knowing that one thing was certain — Sadie the dog could always count on her master, Bill Ojala.

NORTH TO THE POLE

I'D HEARD OF but never met Will Steger of Ely, Minnesota. His name cropped up in newspaper stories, usually in Duluth's *News-Tribune* or in his hometown paper, the *Ely Echo*. Steger was, I gathered, an arctic adventurer with a propensity for pitting himself against the odds. It was reported that he had traveled all across northern Canada by dogsled, and canoed, sometimes alone, along some of the most remote and dangerous rivers in the Arctic.

But now I noticed his name coming up more often. Steger proposed, and I thought without much hope of it ever happening, an assault on the north pole using only dogsleds and skis, without resupply from the air.

My skepticism was a product of years of fending off hopeful adventurers with an idea but no experience or backing. I often had calls from people who wanted me to cover events like their "preparations" for a trip through the jungles of South America or the first bicycle trip around the world. More often than not, the only reason they called me was to try to publicize their idea, and, they hoped, gain them the support they had been unable to foster on their own. By having us produce a story about their efforts, they hoped to gain the credibility they lacked.

I received no such calls from Will Steger. It was a press release from the power company that serves Duluth and St. Louis County that persuaded me to pay a little more attention to Will: "Will Steger and Paul Schurke will be departing Duluth, Minnesota 4th November 1984, to begin a five-thousand mile training run by dog-sled to Barrow, Alaska. The journey would test men, dogs, clothing and equipment in preparation for their scheduled trip to the North Pole in 1986."

So cameraman Don Friedell and I were there on the North Shore of Lake Superior, just east of Duluth, the early winter of 1984, and so was Will Steger.

It was a confused scene that day, as it usually is around sled dogs that are being harnessed for a run. We introduced ourselves to Will Steger, a ruggedly handsome man of about forty, who was surprisingly slight of build for someone who had survived such hardships as his earlier exploits had provided him.

"What about a short interview before you go, Will?" I asked as he snapped the last dog he had lifted out of the truck on a stake-out line. "Sure," said Will. "Where do you want me to stand?" "What about against the truck here with the dogs at your feet," I said, trying to create an interesting picture of the adventurer and his team.

We began the interview with Will explaining that while he would have a variety of different people take turns accompanying him on the upcoming journey, he would go all the way, as would the dogs. It must have been the first time the dogs had heard of the plans for them to pull a sled five thou-

114

sand miles, because the one on Will's left raised its leg and peed all over him. It wasn't exactly champagne, but it did get the training run off to a running start.

Behind a team of "raring to go" dogs, Will and north pole expedition team coleader Paul Schurke shot out along the North Shore Trail headed northeast to the cheers of many well-wishers. Will was going to wind up in Barrow, Alaska, in a few months. In a couple of years, he would wind up at the north pole. And although we didn't know it then, so would we.

We documented Will Steger's adventures as he wound through the far north of Minnesota, across Manitoba, and into the western part of Canada's Northwest Territories. But it was our meeting with him on the Mackenzie River that I remember most vividly.

The rest of the team were waiting for Will outside a small village called Arctic Red River. The location of the settlement marked the confluence of the Arctic Red River and the Mackenzie River. It was midwinter and brutally cold. The team had pitched their tents on the banks of the frozen river and hunkered down to wait for their leader, who was completing the final leg of his five-thousand-mile journey alone. The plan was for the whole group to link up and travel together across the sea ice to Barrow, Alaska. It would be a fitting end to what must have been the longest and most hazardous training run ever for an assault on the north pole.

Will was late. Days late. Don and I were growing frustrated with the long hours sitting in our vehicle with the heater running while the outside temperature hovered around twenty below zero.

I decided we should go look for Will by air. We rented a small aircraft in the town of Inuvik and flew down the white ribbon of ice-covered snow that was the Mackenzie River. It was unmarked. Not an animal or a man had moved in the frigid cold. Recent, unusually heavy snowfalls had left a carpet of virgin snow three feet thick from bank to bank.

We flew fifty miles upstream, when suddenly we saw the string of little black dots that had to be Will and his team of dogs. I instructed the pilot to set the the aircraft down on its skis about a quarter of a mile ahead of Will. This way I knew that our shot of him coming toward us would not be spoiled by marks on the snow in the foreground. We clambered out of the cramped cabin of the single-engine aircraft and sank up to our knees in the powdery, white snow.

I knew immediately that we had placed ourselves in a unique and exciting position. Will was ploughing his way toward us in front of his lead dog, breaking trail for the animals who otherwise would have just floundered in the heavy snow. He had been on the trail alone for a month.

We walked toward him, camera rolling, and I tried to think what words I should use on this momentous occasion. "Will Steger, I presume?" came into my head, but I rejected it as too corny. He was getting close now, so I had to come up with something profound that would be recorded forever on the videotape. I could hear Will's labored breathing as he closed the distance between us. I had to think of something good, something that would be as memorable as Stanley's greeting to Livingstone. I was out of time. I blurted out, "Are you Will Steger?"

Over the next year and a half, we produced a stream of stories about Will's preparations for the expedition to the north pole. He had gathered around him a team of seven people: Paul Schurke from Ely, who would act as coleader; Ann Bancroft from Sunfish Lake, Minnesota, the only woman in the group; Geoff Carroll from Barrow, Alaska; Brent Boddy from Frobisher Bay in the western part of the Canadian Northwest Territories; Richard Weber, a champion cross-country skier from Ottawa, Canada; former Minnesotan and now resident of Alaska "Iron Man" Bob Mantell; and New Zealander Bob McKerrow.

In February 1986, we were all together in Frobisher Bay, which is on Baffin Island in Canada's Northwest Territories, not far from Greenland. The team was fine-tuning their training and equipment before launching the expedition from the very northern tip of Canada's Ellesmere Island, about five hundred miles south of the north pole straight across the frozen Arctic Ocean.

Steger and his intrepid little band of adventurers were going to try to get to the pole by hauling everything they needed on huge dog sleds called komatiks. They would have no support of any kind from the outside world—no food drops, no help with navigation, not even psychological support. Although we planned on flying in to visit them a couple of times during their sixty-day journey, we were under strict instructions not to tell them any news from home. Paul never learned that his one-year-old daughter, Bria, had taken her first steps until he arrived at the north pole, six weeks after this big family event. We were not even allowed to take them mail from their loved ones.

Will Steger was determined to make this epic journey in the same fashion as the only other man ever to have claimed to have done it. In 1986, it was generally recognized that Robert Peary had reached the pole by dog sled in 1909. Steger knew that Perry had all kinds of support during his attempt. He wanted to go one better.

It's ironic that less than two years after Will and Paul led their team successfully to the pole, Peary's claim came under fire, and doubts have been expressed that he ever reached the pole.

But back to Frobisher Bay. It was a full-fledged arctic blizzard. The north pole team had decided to use the inclement weather to test their expedition clothing and themselves by taking a training run through the deserted streets of the town. Don and I were keen to record this, but it was tougher than we thought. Don climbed on the roof of a car, and I drove. Visibility was nil. Complicating matters for me was that not only did I have to try to keep the car on the road, which I couldn't see, but I had to try to keep just ahead of the runners, who disappeared completely if I got more than five yards ahead of them. I drove straight into a ditch within minutes. In the meantime, my brave colleague was trying to stay on the roof of the car and also keep the shadowy figures in the wind and snow in his viewfinder. Later we found we had recorded a very dramatic sequence, but only we knew at what cost.

The training run ended outside the small hotel we were staying at in Frobisher Bay, which, as it turned out, was just as well. I decided to do some quick interviews in the howling winds and blowing snow. The team members were covered in ice. Their faces, where you could see them through their protective masks, were obviously frozen. Their breath came in great clouds of vapor, which was whisked away from them in a flash.

"What better way to train for the north pole?" was Bob McKerrow's rhetorical question.

"It's okay, but I find it's a real problem when my eyelashes freeze together," said Ann, showing us her eyes, which peered through a crusting of ice and snow.

I turned my attention to Geoff Carroll, whose full beard and mustache were a solid sheet of crusted ice from his exhaled breath. "Do you think this is fun?" I asked as he grinned at me through his temporary mask of frosting. "Oh, yes, great fun," he said, and you know, he meant it.

Well, it might have been great fun for the team, but for Don and me, this was work under the worst of circumstances. I still had to videotape my closing statements for the story we would produce for KSTP's news, so we stood, the two of us, in this blizzard, trying to record my summary of the day's events.

"Your nose is frozen." I didn't feel a thing. Ignoring Don's warning, I did several more takes, but he was getting worried. "I'm not kidding. Your nose is frozen, and I mean *really* frozen." His concern finally penetrated the wind and my own vanity, and I sped into the tiny lobby of the nearby hotel. A group of Inuit men sheltering from the storm looked at me, at first as though I was crazy to be out in such weather and then because I had a bright, white growth in the middle of my face that was my nose.

My nose was saved. But now it freezes very quickly if I spend too much time with my face uncovered in sub-zero temperatures. Another price to pay for pursuing people like Will Steger.

The day finally came, the day when the whole team, fifty dogs, and tons of supplies would be loaded on a huge aircraft and flown far north from Frobisher Bay to Resolute, where we would then all be ferried in smaller Twin Otter aircraft to a weather station called Eureka, six hundred miles from the north pole.

Will had told us to be at the airport at seven in the morning. And we were there. It was another one of those typical Frobisher Bay winter days—pitch black, twenty or twenty-five degrees below zero, and with a bitter wind straight out of the north. We were there with our camera at the ready to record the historic loading of the charter aircraft. It was a long day.

The team showed up after several hours with more equipment than the aircraft could possibly carry. The ground staff from Bradley Air decided that because of disputed weights between them and the team leaders, everything that had so far been placed on the aircraft would have to be pulled off again and weighed. The cold was appalling.

I had been aboard the plane to stow our personal bags in the rear part, which had been set up to seat just twelve people: the eight team members, Don and me, and a photographer and reporter from the Minneapolis *Star Tribune*. I saw it was going to be a long, uncomfortable trip. The seats were tiny and close together. With our bags and thick down parkas, I thought we would fill the space entirely, but it was going to be far worse than I imagined.

Late in the afternoon, the bleak greyness that passed for daylight in this part of the world at this time of the year was fading fast. The airline staff were frantic. "If you don't get on the plane and leave right now, you will be here another night," someone yelled above the winds and the howling of a plane load of dogs.

As Don turned his camera on, a distraught Sue Schurke, with her baby daughter slung in the hood of her anorak, was saying a tear-streaked goodbye to her husband, Paul. I clambered up the steps into the passenger compartment. I could barely get in. Apart from the team and the journalists from the newspaper, there were six huge, smelly sled dogs lying on the floor between the seats, and to add insult to injury, one particularly hairy, stinking, but very friendly animal was sitting on my seat. I spent the next twelve hours sitting in my own seat but with my knees under my chin because my sled dog friend was where my feet should be.

In early March, the sun peeks over the horizon for only a few minutes each day when you are standing on the edge of the Arctic Ocean five hundred miles from the north pole. In 1986, it signaled the end of the polar winter and the beginning of a historic expedition.

We had been ferried one hundred miles with the team members, several tons of supplies, and forty-nine sled dogs (one had been inadvertently left in Frobisher Bay) from Eureka to Ward Hunt Island, which was the jumping off point for the trek to the pole.

If there is an end to the earth, it must look like this. An eerie half-light revealed a lunar landscape devoid of life and completely silent.

The Twin Otters had landed us on the sea ice that forever remains bonded to the shore. It was about a mile wide, like a snowy white beach. In the distance, to the north, a huge escarpment rose like a wall across the horizon. It was the pressure ridge that marked where the ever-moving polar ice ground up against the fixed shore ice.

The polar team members went about their work of staking out their dogs and stacking their supplies in a hushed silence. One could catch them swinging their eyes toward the massive barrier in the distance that they knew they would have to cross, starting in just a few hours. To the south, the mountains of Ellesmere Island loomed out of the starlit sky. It was the last land they would see for more than two months.

There were four of us media people with the team. They had their tents; we had the luxury of spending the night in a small hut owned by the Canadian military that had not been occupied for six months or more. The temperature, as best we could tell with a thermometer that only went to forty degrees below zero, was colder than forty degrees below zero.

Paul Schurke put his shoulder against the door of the hut and shoved. Reluctantly, it creaked open to reveal an interior that looked as if it had been last used by Robert Falcon Scott of antarctic fame. In was truly suspended, frozen in time.

But the biggest shock of all was that there were only two bunks, a small table, two chairs, and a kitchen counter. Paul had assured us the cabin was plenty big enough for four media people, their clothing, and their equipment.

Our plane had gone. It wouldn't be back for a day or two. In any case, we had to record the team beginning their journey

121

to the pole. There were four of us and only two narrow bunks. We tossed a coin. My luck was consistent: Don and I would have to sleep on the floor.

While we resolved our sleeping arrangements, Paul had started a small, white-gas camping stove, a tiny thing that in time would melt a pot full of snow to produce water. And that is just what Paul was aiming at. The rest of the team were stacking sacks of dog food on the roof of the cabin, which on the southern exposure had snow drifts to the eaves. *Thump*. The whole building shook from the impact. *Thump*. I looked up as a drift of frost floated down from the ceiling. I don't scare easily. I take chances that others pass up. Some call me reckless, especially when I'm in pursuit of a good story. But at that moment, in that frozen cabin on the Arctic Ocean five hundred miles from the north pole, I was frightened. *Thump*. In my mind's eye, I saw the ceiling collapse. I saw us surviving the destruction of the cabin. What I couldn't see was how we would survive for more than a few hours in temperatures that must have been at least fifty degrees below zero.

But the thumping stopped, the roof held, and the team all crowded into the cabin. There were twelve of us packed into this one room designed for two. With great difficulty, Paul had managed to make the meltwater hot enough to make a weak tea. "Do you want some, Jason?" he asked. "Thanks, Paul," I said, as I reached for the steaming, brimming metal cup he tried to hand to me. It spilled, just a little, and I watched the hot liquid hit the white formica of the little table. I reached out instinctively to wipe up the drops. They were frozen to the table top!

Later, I tried a small experiment. A quarter bottle of brandy froze solid in minutes outside the door of the cabin. I'm sure it would have frozen inside in time. Our audio cables for the microphone were specially made for use in extremely cold weather. They froze here on the Arctic Ocean into plastic-coated steel rods.

We returned to civilization the next day, and the team got on with the preparations to head to the pole. But nearly three weeks later, we were in the air again, in a Twin Otter bound for the team on the ice. They had traveled through the area of pressure ridges and now needed to evacuate a team of dogs they no longer needed. Will said that Robert Peary had fed his excess dogs to the other animals, but in this day and age, to do something like that would enrage too many people. So thousands of dollars had to be spent to send an airplane more than a thousand miles each way to bring a handful of dogs out.

We were to land on the frozen ocean on a flat bit of ice that the team had marked out. Unfortunately, their idea of flat and our pilot's idea of flat were totally different.

Our first try was little more than a touch and go. The skis barely skimmed the snow-covered ice before the pilot pulled back on the stick and put us in the air again. He came around for another try, which was like trying to land on a ploughed field. The Twin Otter was in danger of shaking itself to bits. Back into the air we went.

Our third attempt was almost our last. The plane shuddered and twisted as the skis encountered chunks of ice and snow drifts. It slid sideways and rapidly lost momentum. Knowing if he stopped now he might never get the plane airborne again, the pilot made the decision to use whatever forward movement he still had to try to take off. It seemed like an eternity as the plane plowed through the snow, struggling to get enough lift. Finally, the sound of the engines changed from a screaming protest to a comfortable roar as we soared back into the blue sky.

"We'll make one more try, and that's it," said the pilot, who was cursing those on the surface who had selected such a poor place to land. We have our fourth landing well documented:

123

Don was rolling his large video camera inside the Twin Otter. The picture isn't very steady. In fact, it's all over the place, but that's what it was like inside that airplane.

On the ground, one of the expedition members was filming our descent with an eight-millimeter film camera. The resulting pictures are hair-raising. It was bumpier and noisier than our previous three attempts, but what made it most spectacular was the snowstorm we created with the engines. The airplane wings rocked so savagely that the tips were only inches from the ice. The tail flew in the air, and we shot forward in our seats. But we were down.

On the ice, we found a dispirited team that told of horrific temperatures they estimated had reached an unbelievable seventy-five below. Their faces were covered with scabs from the recurring frostbite. Their lips were cracked as if they had been lost in the desert.

"Iron Man" Bob Mantell was limping suspiciously, but neither he nor anyone else on the team would admit that his feet were severely frostbitten. (He was evacuated on another flight a week later.)

But the sorriest sight of all was the New Zealander, Bob McKerrow. Bob was always the life and soul of the group. Quick-witted and gregarious, he worked hard and happily, using his great strength to its best advantage. But according to Bob, his resilience ran out when a runaway sled crashed into him and injured his back.

"You'd better go talk to Bob. He's pretty upset because he has to go back with you," said Paul. So Don and I carried our equipment over to Bob, who was looking as dejected as I'd ever seen any man. He had a large white strap around the middle of his bright red parka, presumably to ease the pain of the back injury.

"Ah, feeling very sad," he said in reply to my greeting. "A little bitter, you know. You put two years into preparation

124

and you get crushed by a sled." Bob's eyes filled with tears, and they ran down the jagged course of his scabbed face and frozen beard. I noticed his nose was so badly frostbitten that one nostril had turned black. "I have hurt my back. It's really debilitating. It's hard to leave," he said.

"Why? Is it because you are not realizing your ambition? Or is it the friends you are leaving on the ice?" I asked. "Ah," he sighed. "It's not ambition. I don't think ambition is important, it's the close friendships and," he sobbed, "there's a sense of letting people down." We did indeed take Bob McKerrow back to civilization with us. X rays showed no serious damage to his back, and he quickly recovered.

The team had many adventures on their way to the north pole. The story is theirs, and it is well told in a book called *North to the Pole*, written by Will Steger and Paul Schurke.

We gathered towards the end of April in Resolute and waited, waited for the call that would tell us that the team had reached the pole.

We knew they were very close. A radio transmitter they carried told us, via satellite, almost exactly where they were. Oddly, they themselves didn't have this information. They were totally dependent on Paul's skill as a navigator, using a traditional sextant to read the angle of the sun above the horizon. Finally the call came. A weak radio transmission, Paul's voice saying, "We're at the pole. We're at the pole."

By now, there were three plane loads of people waiting to go the pole to meet the team, and all three planes took off immediately. It took twelve hours to get there, with a stop at the weather station Eureka for fuel and then a bizarre landing on a remote lake called Hazen, where the planes unloaded several fifty-five gallon drums of fuel, the pilots hand-pumped the fuel into the aircraft's tanks, and we took off again.

The north pole was featureless. Not surprising, since it is

125

only a shell of ice on a very deep ocean. But it was astounding to fly so far for so long across the trackless ice to suddenly come across a scattering of black dots that could only be Will and his intrepid group.

The final irony was that this difficult and dangerous journey ended like a Sunday school picnic. The planes landed without incident. The sun was shining, and the temperature was ten degrees *above* zero. The team members were in high spirits, and a couple of hours were spent taking photographs and conducting interviews. Pretty soon, it was all over and time for everyone, dogs included, to be loaded into the Twin Otters, which had one of their engines running the whole time we were there. Arctic pilots do not shut their aircraft down when they are a thousand miles from the nearest mechanic.

As we rose into the air over the north pole, I leaned over the back of the pilot's seat and noticed the automatic compass was showing a heading of 180 degrees. Trying to show off my knowledge of geography and the points of the compass, I said, "I see we are flying due south." The pilot never flinched, he just snorted, "That's the only direction you can fly from here!"

THE DOG LADY OF
ESKO

IT WAS A call from the St. Louis County Humane Society that led us to the "Dog Lady of Esko." The woman who called my office during the winter of 1985 wasn't sure if Mrs. Hautaluoma would be receptive to a television crew visiting her old farm, but she urged us to try. "She is very unusual," my caller said. "She's seventy-five years old and toughs it out all alone since her husband died, and not only that, she takes in any dog she finds or people dump on her."

Well, Idia Hautaluoma may be a loner, but she does have a phone. "I don't know why you'd be interested in me," she said. "I'm just an old woman who lives alone with a few dogs."

She's easy to find, Idia Hautaluoma. The road she lives on is called Hautaluoma Road. And that's part of the problem. Apparently, the word is out locally that if you have a dog you don't want it's simple to just dump it on Hautaluoma Road, where, you can be sure, it will be well taken care of.

It was a bitterly cold day when we drove down Hautaluoma Road. The only sign of life was a small figure bundled up in a short black coat, wearing a bright yellow wool hat and a pair of those cheap gloves you can buy in the hardware store for about two dollars. Scattered around her heels were half a dozen dogs of all shapes and sizes. It was, of course, Idia. And she was plodding along on an old pair of wooden skis, her boots flopping around under the worn leather straps that were the bindings.

This seventy-five-year-old woman had a rope around her left wrist, and it was attached to a large black plastic bag that dragged along the snow-covered road behind her. Wisps of grey hair stuck out from under her hat, and her ruddy face shone with exertion.

We had found Idia during one of her regular but difficult journeys to the local food store, where she buys bones and scrap meat for ten cents a pound. Even at that, we knew that Idia was spending a third of her social security check on food for the dogs. But she brushed off our question by saying, "I really live quite simply, and I'm satisfied to do that. I'm not one of these people who have to have caviar or something."

She laughed merrily at her own little joke as she began a fire under an old grating by a lean-to outside the house. On the grating, she placed a huge pot that was obviously years old and had seen better days. As we all stood waiting for the water to boil, I looked at the house, which was surrounded by so many odds and ends it was difficult to see where the entrance was. Everything was covered with two feet of snow, and we were not surprised to learn that the homestead had no running water or central heating.

As steam started to rise from the water in the pot, Idia started jamming huge bones into it. She was in the process of making dog-food stew. "The bones and cornmeal are cheap, and they make a fine meal for the dogs," she said.

And dogs there were. The smell of food cooking had conjured up about a dozen animals that snuffled around the three of us and the bubbling pot. They were a motley lot, big and small, black and brown, some with a touch of identifiable breed in them, others real mutts.

"We started out with only one or two dogs, and we gradually found we had more and more." Idia was talking about how it all started when she and her husband used to farm this marginal land near Esko, Minnesota. But he had been dead since 1971. "Of course, now I enjoy the company. There's also the one year I had a bear here. It felt nice to have about six big dogs around."

Idia didn't have to worry about ever being lonely if she found dogs good company. There were plenty of people who were prepared to drop their unwanted animals off at the end of the road marked Hautaluoma.

With the help of the Humane Society, Idia had whittled down her collection of dogs from a high of thirty to about twenty animals when we visited her. She said she was determined to hang on to at least ten. "The reason I keep that many is I've lost so many dogs. Last year around Thanksgiving, three of my dogs disappeared. So, you know, I figure if I have a little cushion, then they won't all be gone at once."

RACCOONS MAKE
LOUSY PETS

WE WERE A long way from home. Oriska, North Dakota, is way west of Fargo, but the story we sought there was intriguing.

Gary and Sharon Dahl were longtime residents of this small town, and they may have lived their lives in perfect anonymity but for their unusual choice of pets.

When cameraman Duane Rude and I arrived at the little white house on the edge of Oriska, the first thing we heard was something being beaten. It wasn't the pets . . . it was eggs. A couple of dozen eggs, their shells scattered in the sink as Sharon beat the blazes out of the interiors. It was breakfast time for the pets, and the eggs would go with two pounds of dog food, a dozen cookies, and a box of Fruit Loops.

As if on cue, two animals came through a flap cut in the living room wall. They were biggest raccoons I'd ever seen.

In the wild, a well-fed raccoon may reach a healthy thirty pounds. Custer (raccoon humongous number one) weighed

131

over fifty pounds, and Cooter (raccoon gigantic number two) went a distinctly unhealthy sixty-two pounds. I say unhealthy without any veterinarian backing—just watching these fat animals waddle across the floor was justification enough for my amateur diagnosis.

They may have been overweight, but they were loved. Gary and Sharon were devoted to Custer and Cooter. As we all stood in a little circle around the animals, watching them gorge themselves on breakfast, Sharon admitted that raccoons aren't everyone's idea of a good pet. "No, they are not. But we raised them, and we are attached to them. If we let them go now, they would just die."

She didn't exaggerate. As I watched these gluttons ram the food down their throats with both hands, I guessed there wasn't enough food outside this house to keep them happy. Gary said proudly, "They eat until they drop from exhaustion."

A true animal lover could, I suppose, teeter on the edge of bankruptcy to keep these raccoons amply fed, but it certainly took two very special people to put up with their other habits.

You had to be in the house awhile for it to sink in. There was hardly any furniture, and what there was, was strictly utilitarian, almost institutional. As Gary lay on the rug in the largely empty living room, one of the raccoons worked hard to find a piece of candy he had in his jeans pocket. "They destroy everything they get their hands on," he said. Now it made sense. That's why the place was so sparsely furnished. They used to have furniture—lamps, plants, the whole bit. I know because Gary showed me a photo album with snaps of their house as it used to be. It was all they had to remind them of what life was like preraccoon.

"You can't have anything new," he said. "They tear the couch up and tear all the furniture up. They destroy everything." I looked at Gary in amazement. Such devotion. Most

132

people I knew would be tempted to have their kids exterminated if they wreaked this kind of havoc.

I asked him about the raccoons' sanitary habits. He said they were "sort of" house trained, whatever that meant. So far I hadn't heard any redeeming features about these animals that the Dahls doted on. "Do they have a good side, Gary?" I asked. "They are very lovable," he replied, as he fought with a sixty-pound eating machine that was trying to get a candy he had clenched between his lips. "They are either very playful or very lovable. Now, they are playful," he said, giving up the tidbit before the animal ate his face.

The last we saw of Custer and Cooter was their wide rumps as one followed the other through the flap in the wall into their den where, Gary and Sharon assured us, they would soon recover from the strain of eating breakfast.

Sharon stood up and headed for the kitchen. Time to start getting lunch.

THE WILDERNESS
FAMILY

SPRING COMES LATE and slowly to Minnesota's north country.
So we were not surprised in late April to find lots of snow still
covering the old logging road that we bounced along on our
way to visit the Hecker family.

I had read a story in the Duluth *News-Tribune* about a
remarkable family that lived deep in the woods near Finland,
Minnesota. True to type, they had no telephone, and as we always liked to ask people if we could produce a television feature story about them, I had a problem. How was I going to
reach this reclusive group that, the newspaper story made
clear, did not have a lot of truck with the outside world?

Finland, Minnesota, is a small town lying in the hills about
ten miles from the shore of Lake Superior. It's so small that my
state map doesn't give a population count. My only clue was
a reference in the newspaper story to some babysitting duties
performed by one of the Hecker daughters for the owners of
a gas station in Finland.

135

With nothing to lose and everything to gain, I placed a long-distance call to the gas station. "Hi, this is Jason Davis of KSTP-TV in Minneapolis. I'm trying to get in touch with a family I believe you know." I knew it was a long shot, and from experience I expected to have to spend a good deal of time explaining why I wanted to reach the family. But this was my lucky day.

"You want to talk to the Heckers?" The response didn't have the incredulous edge I had expected. And then, "Just a sec, Mrs. Hecker is right here." "Hello." It seemed I had called just as the matriarch of the family, Johanna Hecker, had dropped by the gas station to pick up her daughter, who had been babysitting for the owners for the past couple of days.

And that's how I made contact with this group of people whose contact with the rest of us was limited to an occasional visit to a tiny town that didn't even rate a population number on the state map.

The road grew progressively worse. Our four-wheel-drive vehicle was throwing up sheets of meltwater and mud as we plunged deeper into the pine woods. The directions that Johanna had given me, after saying they would all be delighted to see us any time we chose, went something like this, "Take the first left after you get into town and keep going for about twenty miles." Problem was, the track that passed for a road in these parts tended to fork at irregular intervals, and we had to make several instinctive choices along the way.

We should have been suspicious when we spotted signs nailed to trees that read:

We knew the family we sought valued their privacy, but we also knew they were friendly and hospitable. A sign on a tree said:

TRESPASSERS
WILL BE SHOT

It didn't sound right somehow.

The road deteriorated into two crazy ruts that had obviously been made by a tractor or some other piece of heavy equipment. It suddenly just ended at the front of a log house. A couple of old cars and some big yellow machines lay about, and a man and a woman were walking toward the home. It was the first sign of life we had seen for over an hour, but to our astonishment, they just kept walking, ignoring us completely. "Hi, Hi," I yelled. They appeared to hear me because I noticed their backs stiffen, but they never broke their stride. "Hey, excuse me." I was becoming impossible to ignore, and reluctantly, the woman turned and faced our car. "Is this the Hecker residence?" I asked, knowing that if it was, we were not as welcome as we had expected to be. "Who?" The woman's attitude was completely without charm. "No, you took a wrong fork about a mile back," she said, after I repeated my question. With that, she stumbled away across the muddy ruts that formed the front yard and disappeared into the house in the woods.

What makes this anecdote so interesting is the sharp contrast between the natural enmity of the people we visited accidently and the friendliness of the ones we were on our way to see on purpose.

We knew it was, without doubt, the right place when we

turned a bend and across the road was a handmade wooden arch with these words burned into the center:

A little farther on, nailed to a balsam fir:

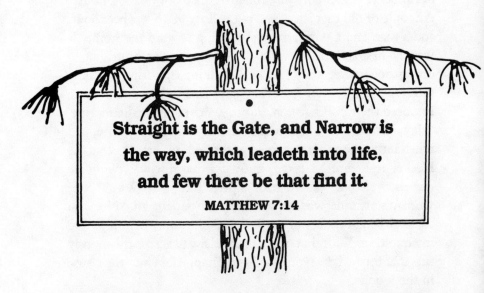

Straight is the Gate, and Narrow is the way, which leadeth into life, and few there be that find it.
MATTHEW 7:14

This was to us, and to anyone else who cared to call, the first introduction to the world of David and Johanna Hecker, their large family, and their thousand acres of a place like nowhere else on earth.

The sun was shining, and the boughs of the millions of fir

138

trees were weighed down with brilliant white snow. The road wound through this enchanted forest that just a short time ago seemed so forbidding and now, probably because of the friendly and peaceful nature of the signs, seemed to beckon us on.

Cameraman Tim Jones and I saw her at the same instant. Her bright red dress stood out starkly against the green and white of the forest. She was about eight years old, her hair a multitude of braids piled up in an old-fashioned but very attractive way. The dress went to her ankles, and the high collar and sleeves were trimmed with lace. Her wide, dark eyes matched those of the deer that stood beside her as she stroked its back.

I couldn't get Tim out of the car quick enough to record this incredible scene. As he struggled to get his camera out and balance it for the light conditions under the trees, I asked the little girl her name. "Beth," she said, unsmiling but immensely curious about our obvious interest in her. "Beth Hecker?" I asked, knowing it could be no other. She nodded in an absent-minded kind of way as she watched Tim, who by now was pointing his camera straight at her and her furry friend. The deer's name, it turned out, was Wetzel.

I heard them before I saw them, the jangle of harness, the shouts of men, and the snorting of horses. From a trail that led deep into the woods, two huge draft horses came pulling the largest sled I'd ever seen. At the reins was a big man with a full grey beard.

This, it turned out, was David Hecker, a sixty-two-year-old native of Los Angeles, who after spending eight years living a simple life as a missionary in Guatemala decided that modern America was not to his liking. He and his family tried for success as a gospel singing group. They roamed the country and were eventually good enough to appear on television. But they always dreamed of settling down on their own place

139

where they could live in the way that would make them happiest.

In 1978, during one of the worst winters on record in this northern part of the United States, the Heckers began to carve a clearing for a home on a thousand acres of virgin forest. Nine years later, we stood with our camera to record what progress this unusual family had made in their search for their version of utopia.

"Jump on up," yelled David, as the huge sled came level to where we were standing with Beth and her friend Wetzel. I jumped on the lumbering sled to join three other men, all bearded, dressed in rough work clothes and looking about as friendly as could be. The sled was piled with bales of hay that the men began to unload when the sled shuddered to a halt outside a huge wooden house standing on a rocky outcrop at the end of the trail.

A ramp led up to the door, which was about ten feet up to accommodate the storage space under the house. We were still recording the scene, which appeared to us to have been lifted straight out of an episode of "Little House on the Prairie," when a handsome woman of about fifty, dressed in a floor-length dress and a colorful apron, called, "Come on up, the table's set for all of you."

Any self-respecting film director would have been proud of the scene that met our eyes when we walked up the ramp into the warmth of the house. We found ourselves at the far end of what was one huge room. It must have stretched away for sixty feet to the big windows at the other end. Although there were no walls, the space was divided naturally into a cooking and eating area; a large workspace that housed a loom, with a blanket or rug work in progress, and a spinning wheel; and at the end by the windows, a lounge area with several comfortable-looking chairs and couches. The far left-hand corner housed the one incongruous item, a full-sized grand piano. Where we stood was midway between an area on our right that although there was no running water contained two large kitchen sinks and considerable counter space and an area on our left that contained a long trestle table with place settings for sixteen. A dozen people were either milling around or already seated. It was a noisy, happy place.

Johanna, the woman who had issued the invitation to eat, was bustling around directing her five daughters and one daughter-in-law what to prepare and what to serve. Her four sons and one grandson were already seated with two visiting friends, men in their sixties, who, as far as we could tell, were just like family.

Suddenly, the noise stopped. Apart from the whimpering of eleven-month-old grandson Noah, the room was silent. "Father, I want to tell you one more time that I'm grateful for your love for us and for your watch-care." David's deep voice boomed around the rough wooden walls and echoed down the length of the room. "I thank you for how you show your blessings to us, and I thank you for this food." Other than eight-year-old Beth, who couldn't resist a mischievous smile, everyone at the table had their heads bowed over their plates. "Bless it, strengthen our bodies with it, I pray, in Jesus' name. Amen."

David's eyes snapped open as if he was trying to catch someone who wasn't sufficiently grateful for the food. He had dark eyes, deep with intelligence, faith, and love. And there was something else. The eyes said, "I am the law here. Who among you will challenge me?"

The cast-iron ladle sunk into the thick soup and came up brimming and steaming before being slowly poured into the earthenware bowls that sat in front of more than a dozen hungry people. Twenty-year-old Rachel carved thick slices of homemade bread on a wooden board. Rachel, like her sisters Becky, who was fourteen, Deborah, fifteen, and Joanna, twenty-four, was wearing a long, obviously but beautifully homemade dress.

Their parents made no mistake when they insisted their daughters should never cut their hair or wear pants. These Hecker girls were stunning. They had a beauty that surely had a lot to do with the way they lived. They had flawless skin and slender bodies. And unlike many of their peers in the world outside this wilderness home of theirs, they were modest and graceful.

The Heckers are, to the best of their ability, self-sufficient. A single cow provides all the milk they need. Vegetables, grown during the kinder times of the year, last all winter in a root cellar. Horses and sheep provide power, meat, and wool. And only a hundred and fifty feet from the house, a few swift cranks on a pump handle brings up ice-cold, crystal-clear water.

"The rock music doesn't come in here. Our children are not in the public school." David was explaining what they had and what they didn't miss by living off the beaten track. "We are making the input in our children's growing minds. Not someone else." Again the glaring challenge flashed in David's eyes. I gathered he thought we were skeptical of him and his motives. I was careful to assure him we were simply fascinated with his seemingly idyllic homestead and family.

Dinner was over, and most of the family had drifted to the far end of the room to pick up the evening's activities. As the girls began to clear the table, I asked Johanna if she missed modern conveniences in her kitchen. "I have four or five automatic dishwashers, and they all work by remote control." Her eyes twinkled behind her rimless spectacles. "All I have to do is speak the words, and they go to work." She was right. Quietly and efficiently, the older girls were erasing the signs that a large group of people had just devoured a couple of gallons of stew and several loaves of bread.

Little Beth was sitting at her father's side on a well-used couch under the window. A worn Bible was in his huge hands, and the child sat spellbound as he gave the text his own words. "You can see here how many times you have to forgive a brother or sister if they do something unkind to you." Beth nodded gravely, her dark eyes unblinking as she listened to her father. "Jesus says you have to tell 'em they're forgiven."

Diagonally across the room, oldest son Nathan sat with his wife, Renae, who was holding their eleven-month-old son, Noah. We moved the camera across, adjusted our portable light, and tried to learn more about how Nathan found his wife and why he stayed with his family.

Nathan, who was twenty-five years old, told us that he had met his wife at a religious seminar. Renae, who was twenty-two, had grown up in an affluent suburb of Minneapolis. When she was nineteen, this unusual young woman had asked her parents to select a husband for her. Nathan Hecker was their choice. Neither Nathan nor Renae had dated before they met. In fact, Nathan said, "The first woman I ever kissed was my wife, and that was on my wedding night."

He went on to tell us about their life so far on the thousand acres. Their first child, a daughter named Ruth, died four days after her premature birth. Then, when Noah was only a couple of months old, lightning set their hand-built house on fire, and it burned to the ground as they watched. Without rancor, Nathan showed us a photograph of his home in flames. His calm attitude reflected the philosophy of them all. David said they were a "Christ centered" family, and their religion was their strength. Nathan was proof.

But what of his beautiful sisters? What would be their fate? Well, as you may have guessed, their father had a thing or two to say about that. "The fact is, one of the requirements is anybody who marries my children has to be debt free!" His voice rose as he propounded his rules. "There is a thousand acres here. Any son-in-law can build his house."

There was no doubt about what would be expected of any young man who braved the twenty miles of bad roads to woo a Hecker girl. But should he persist, he would be getting a very accomplished young woman. The Hecker girls could hold their own with their peers in all academic subjects. They could cook and sew. They were, without exception, good looking, and they could all sing and play music.

As the sun set over the pine tops to the west, Johanna lit several kerosene lanterns. The warm, soft glow illuminated the whole family as they gathered around the big piano in the corner.

Beginning with the deep bass tones of Nathan, they sang:

There's a sweet, sweet spirit in this place.
And I know that it's the spirit of the Lord.

All of them, with the exception of baby Noah, came in on the melody, perfectly in tune, on this wistful, plaintive hymn that for us was the perfect end to a wonderful story.

In the television piece, the sounds of the family singing faded under Johanna's voice as she said, "I'll never feel sorry that I lived here. I never wished I lived somewhere else. I've always been glad that this was home and I was home. It's a real tranquil way of life."

A FRIEND IN TIME

HAVE YOU EVER stopped to wonder who it is that gets up early enough each day to make sure your favorite cafe has fresh soup, stews, and things like stroganoff as early in the day as eleven-thirty in the morning?

When we first met fifty-five-year-old Lorraine Schultz, it was a little after eight o'clock in the morning, but she had been at work since two.

Lorraine is one of those people you hardly ever see. She is a cook, and a good one too, at the Front Street Cafe in Brainerd, Minnesota. For all of her fifty-five years, Lorraine lived among the rest of us, and hardly anyone noticed. She never married and never sought the limelight, content to just go about her business, work hard, and be nice to people.

When we met her, she was standing over a huge pot, ladle in hand, her glasses all steamed up, happily stirring up the ingredients of the soup of the day—vegetable, as I recall.

I guess we could have easily produced a television feature

story about this dedicated woman who had faithfully toiled at her choice of work for so long. We were told that among her other attributes, she was always at work on time. Well, the reason we had come to meet her *was* time. Lorraine had a thing about time. In fact, her second-floor apartment in an aged house not far from downtown was a sort of shrine to time.

You could hear them before you saw them. As we climbed the stairs, a kind of white noise drifted down. It was difficult to describe. After all, how many people have heard Lorraine's timepieces — all six hundred of them?

Every inch of every wall and all flat surfaces carried clocks. Everywhere we looked, the time of day stared back at us. Clocks to the left of us, clocks to the right of us, on the floor and hanging from the ceiling.

"I try to keep them all going all the time," said Lorraine, unaware of the pun. "I have the biggest problem when daylight saving comes around. It takes several days to get them all changed."

The remarkable thing about Lorraine's collection of clocks was that none of them were in the least bit valuable. They were inexpensive, mostly plastic, and probably inaccurate. There wasn't a collector's item among them.

But did Lorraine care? "I like my grandfather clock. I like my Mickey Mouse clock. I like all my clocks. I just love to watch them and listen to them."

Lorraine's bedroom was, like every other room in the small apartment, wall-to-wall clocks. Plastic owls swung their eyes once a second. Dolls with clocks on their stomachs grinned from the shelves. Even baseball caps had second hands sweeping around just above the peaks.

And all the while, the sound. You'd have to visit her yourself to appreciate the massed ticking of six hundred clocks. But, she said, not only did the noise not bother her, it was

146

positively soothing. Remember, Lorraine had to be at work at two in the morning.

When she told us she had to be in bed each night at seven-thirty, we suggested she would have no trouble knowing when to retire. "No. No trouble at all," she said. "And I've never been late for work either."

MINNESOTA BY THANKSGIVING

"JASON, COULD YOU come here a minute." News director Stan Turner motioned me into his office, which had one glass wall facing the bustling newsroom at KSTP. "What now?" I wondered. Had a member of the public complained about my treatment of a story? Was there a question about my time sheet for last week? After all, I had put down a legitimate three hours of overtime for covering that fire downtown on Tuesday evening. Maybe it was the eight dollar expense I had incurred buying that album of steam engine sound effects for a story about a new fun railroad that was starting up in Stillwater, Minnesota.

"We want you to go to Indonesia to find a refugee family and bring them back," Stan said. "How soon can you leave?" To say I was stunned at the question would be an understatement. I stared at Stan as though he had just materialized in front of my eyes. "Jason, did you hear me?" Stan asked. "Mr. Hubbard [the owner of KSTP] wants you to find a family that has two sons already here and bring them back by Thanksgiving. The boys and their aunt were sponsored by the Memorial Lutheran Church in Afton, and apparently the Hubbard family has connections with that church."

Things happened fast. KSTP helicopter pilot Roger Greenan was put on the first plane to Singapore to get the ball rolling. Roger had spent several years flying helicopters in that region of the Far East, and his contacts would prove to be invaluable. I set to work arranging visas and travel documents for myself, videotape cameraman Gary Hill, and sound man Phil Engelstad.

This would be the first trip into such exotic locales for Gary and Phil, and the initial thing for them to do was suffer. I only had to have booster shots, but for those two, the visit to the clinic at the University of Minnesota Hospital would prove to be a painful experience. We had no idea where this trip would lead us in our search for the Vietnamese family we knew had escaped from South Vietnam several months before. We also knew that they were being held by the Indonesian authorities. What we didn't know was exactly where we would find them in the archipelago that formed this nation in the China Sea. We did recognize the need for more health protection than might be needed for a trip to Miami. We started off with typhoid and cholera shots in the upper arm. Bared butts took the stab of a needle that introduced the minute slug of liquid called gamma globulin, which we hoped would protect us all from the ravages of dysentery. And with some relief, we accepted chloroquine tablets that would stave off malaria. Gary and Phil were pleasantly surprised that the initial pain of the shots wore off quickly, and they continued to pack the hundreds of pounds of equipment we would take twelve thousand miles around the world with us in search of one family named Ly.

The next morning, I met two young men at Minneapolis–St. Paul International Airport who looked as if their arms were locked stiffly at an angle of about twenty degrees away from their bodies. Both Gary and Phil told of feeling feverish, of lumps like golf balls under the armpits, and of angry red lesions where the needle had scratched their upper arms.

As sick as they felt, it wasn't enough to dampen our enthusiasm for this great adventure. Roger had called from his base in Singapore and said the Indonesian authorities had assured him we could find and bring back the family we sought in time for the Thanksgiving holiday ten days away. It was an important point. KSTP was prepared to foot the cost of the whole operation, but the company is in business to cover news and produce interesting features that would attract audiences away from its competitors. Eleven-year-old Vu Anh Le and his brother Liem, who was nine, had escaped from South Vietnam with their aunt on the last American ship to leave there after the fall of Saigon. They now lived in Afton, Minnesota, with their aunt and her husband. What a coup it would be if we could find their father and mother and their two siblings: brother Tuan Anh, who was ten, and little sister Yen Hai, who they had never seen because she was only five years old. They had been separated for longer than that.

It was a long journey. From the Twin Cities, we chased the sunset in our Northwest Airlines DC-10 to Seattle. From Seattle we flew to Narita Airport near Tokyo, Japan, where we changed planes to fly to Hong Kong. Then, after an overnight stay, we went on to Singapore.

After clearing customs in Singapore, in itself no mean feat, arriving as we did with about a hundred thousand dollars worth of tape and film equipment, much of it labeled "Made in Japan," we staggered out into the humidity and clamor of one of the world's most glamorous and colorful cities. Roger Greenan immediately took charge of the situation. By nature a "can do" sort of guy, he was in his element. A stocky man of medium height, he was dressed appropriately in khaki pants and shirt and strutted like a bantam rooster through the crowds of Asians thronging the airport concourse alternately trying to tell us what progress he had made and barking orders like a drill sergeant at the porters and taxi drivers who pestered us continuously for our business . . . and our dollars.

This booming city, so long a crucial trading point at the crossroads of the world, teemed with life. Like other places in the region, it posed the visual challenge of absorbing abject poverty and sheer opulance in the same sweep of the eyes. Glistening office blocks stretched into the sky, drawing attention away from the flimsy shacks with dirty children adorning the stoops that displayed pitiful washing on poles out of the windows like flags of surrender.

Following a series of "don't mess me about, buddy, I know my way around" instructions from Roger, our cabs, with bottomed-out rear springs from the weight of our gear in the trunk, finally jerked to a stop outside our hotel. We were not about to rough it, at least as long as we were in Singapore. The Mandarin Hotel climbed from the enormous lobby at street level fifty stories above Singapore. Our rooms were luxurious and far above the dusty, noisy streets. A look out of the window revealed a panorama of harbor, city, suburbs, and a second giant tower of the hotel under construction, also fifty stories and encased in a labyrinth of bamboo scaffolding five hundred feet from top to bottom, with every inch of the flimsy-looking network of bamboo lashed together with rope. Like ants, the hundreds of workers clambered around this lacework, as surefooted as you could be while barefoot on a three-inch stem of a jungle plant that is obviously cheaper in Singapore than steel tubing.

Over a glass of delicious lemonade in the cavernous lobby cafe, Roger briefed us on his progress in locating the Ly family and the status of our applications for visas to enter Indonesia. "It will take a few more days, but I have discovered a way to move things along despite the fact that I have strict instructions from KSTP not to bribe anyone," Roger said. Roger had worked several years before as partner with an Indonesian businessman named Wibisono. There are only two men in Indonesia named Wibisono: Roger's friend and an admiral. Roger found that when he mentioned his friend Wibisono to the military bureaucrats, things happened much faster.

But not fast enough. We found we had a couple of days with little to do but wait. Fortunately, that wasn't a hard thing to do, since we were staying in a superluxury hotel in one of the world's most cosmopolitan cities. One memorable evening was spent at a unique Singapore institution called Newton's Circus. Newton's Circus is, in fact, a circus in the English tradition, an open space at the vortex of traffic where several roads all come together. In Singapore, Newton's Circus is, by day, a parking lot around which converging traffic swirls to transfer from one major city thoroughfare to another. At night, Newton's Circus undergoes a metamorphosis, changing within an hour from a parking lot, from which the office workers have fled, into an open-air, loosely structured, many-faceted, multiracial restaurant.

Roger led us across town like a general leading his troops. Our company of four arrived, breathless and hungry, at what he promised would be the gastronomic treat of our lives. You could see and smell the cluster of cooking places long before you reached them. There was a glow in the air that flared like sun spots, shadowy figures appeared and disappeared in blooms of steam, a steady chatter in a variety of tongues seemed to reach a crescendo just before something splashed into a red-hot wok with a spitting hiss. It was like a dragon's convention here in the heart of Singapore.

We stepped hesitantly into the center of this collection of

153

entrepreneurs, who were as much hustling salesmen of their culinary delights as they were cooks. "See here, fresh crabs, Sir." A Malaysian stall owner beckoned us over to peer into a large plastic bucket swarming with the red armored legs of live crabs.

It was hot. The natural humidity of this tropical city continues through the evenings. The steam of dozens of portable frying plates, woks, and boiling pots filled the air with a pungent moisture that seemed to clog the nostrils and even satisfy, to some extent, the pangs of hunger that surged back and forth as we wandered among the stalls. Take your choice. Satay from Malaysia, Chinese dishes full of spicy meats and crisp vegetables, Indian curries, yellow and oily, full of the promise of a scorched tongue and reamed-out sinuses, Pakistani dishes of unknown ingredients prepared and served by a beautiful woman marred only by the rivulets of perspiration coursing down her unblemished cheeks. Baby squid, lobster, bowls of steaming boiled and fried rice, lamb and goat in thin strips, seasoned and cooked on slivers of bamboo. We sat in the center of the stalls and dined like kings on dishes that came at us from every side and washed it all down with quart bottles of beer brewed in Kuala Lumpur. It was a brief, enjoyable respite and a fitting introduction to the Far East. The next morning, we picked up our visas, which would enable us to travel to Indonesia to try to find and recover the Vietnamese refugee family Ly, who we wanted to bring back like a trophy to Minnesota — by Thanksgiving.

With the all-important official stamp on a page in our passports, we were free to travel to where we thought the family might be. Tanjungpinang is the main town on the Indonesian island of Pulau Bintan, which lies about fifty miles south and east of Singapore across the Strait of Malacca. It's all part of the South China Sea, and as we went to buy our tickets for the boat trip across, I was excited to see these exotic waters that for centuries had been plied by pirates, smugglers, buccaneers, merchantmen, and fishermen of every nationality on earth that ever built a boat.

If it wasn't very organized at the little shipping office on the dock of Singapore Harbor before we arrived with our stacks of cases and boxes of equipment, it was chaos shortly after we got there. "Do you want to go on the express boat?" The clerk was quite pleasant, and we nodded in unison that certainly we wanted to go on their fastest and, by definition, their finest boat. "Okay, where is your luggage?" The clerk looked stunned as we directed our porters to dump this mountain of material in front of his desk. "Excuse me, Sir," he said politely to Roger. "There will be a large amount of money coming from you for excess baggage."

Now it was our turn to look like four dead fish. Our mouths hung open with amazement, and our eyes widened in unison at our not-too-genuine shock. We are practiced at this maneuver. It is standard routine at every airline counter we approach, grossly overloaded and anxious to avoid the unpleasantness of spending more money than is absolutely necessary. Almost as one, Roger and I launched into a heartfelt wailing, pleading with the stone-faced clerk the poverty of our company and the extremely good deed for mankind that our mission entailed. What I thought would bring tears to the eyes of the sphinx had no discernible effect on the mask of unconcern that was the clerk's face. It dawned on us that this was the wrong approach, so we did the next most sensible thing. I shouted and Roger banged his meaty fist on the clerk's desk. Apparently, this was the method that worked in this little cluttered steamship office in Singapore. The clerk said nothing as he dug in a drawer and came up with a sheaf of tickets. Peeling four off, he handed them to us and waved us away. We walked out of the office glowing with triumph. We'd shown them that we were not babes in the wood, easy pickings for the far eastern version of the good old American rip-off.

"Carry your bags, Sir?" The question came from a tiny, wizened old man who looked as if he would blow away in a stiff breeze. He was completely bald but sported a long, Mandarin-type mustache. Dark even for an Asian, he was dressed in a thin singlet that only served to accentuate his bony shoulders and upper arms and a tattered pair of blue shorts that looked as if they had been washed a thousand times. He was barefoot. There we stood, not one of us over forty, healthy, well fed, and, by and large, in good physical shape, but too smart to carry our own bags if someone else would do it for a fair price.

Roger haggled with the little guy because he would have thought we were stark raving mad if we didn't, agreed on a price (less than five dollars), and motioned him to start hauling. Some of the equipment cases weighed over ninety pounds, and we were astounded to see the freelance porter hoist those suckers on his back and carry them. Our amazement grew when we saw that he had to carry them up a flight of a dozen steps, across a bridgeway, and then down a dozen steps to the other side. The fact that we simply walked a hundred feet on a level platform to reach the same place as our luggage was bound for was a mystery we never solved.

Finally, everything and everybody was loaded on the rather battered old boat that was bound for the port of Tanjungpinang. We carried no food or drink, but since we had paid a premium to take the fast boat, we only expected to be at sea for about two hours. It was crowded, and we had to push our way along the narrow passageways to get from the bow to the stern so Gary and Phil could aim the camera and microphone at me as I stood precariously on the cabin roof describing what we were doing. It would look very dramatic when shown in Minnesota, I thought, as I told of our quest leading us across the Strait of Malacca and the South China Sea. What color, what drama. This was the stuff of James Bond and Herman Melville. Finished with recording my commentary, I stood at the rail and watched the parade of boats and ships from the four corners of the world that funneled through this narrow, strategic channel joining the Indian Ocean with the Pacific. So busy is this stretch of salt water that a towering control building rises from a rocky promontory near Singapore Harbor housing a group of people who, twenty-four hours a day, three hundred and sixty-five days a year, act as shipping control officers. By radio, they instruct pilots on which course to take through the straits and into or out of the harbor.

I stood transfixed. Memories of my former days as a British merchant seaman came flooding back as I watched the sampans, junks, fishing boats, freighters, and ponderous oil tankers ply these romantic waters that still, we were told with relish by an English-speaking passenger, carried the hulls of pirate ships that preyed on the weak and unwary. I was deep in reverie when Gary looked at his watch and said, "Shouldn't we have been there by now?" We had been at sea for nearly three hours, and the only sight of land was a palm-tree-lined coast about five miles off our starboard side.

The four of us looked at each other, and the light of understanding flowed into our eyes like the sun coming up in the morning. The clerk who sold us our tickets had had the last laugh. We had not paid excess baggage fees — we were also *not* on the fast boat.

More than four hours after leaving Singapore, we approached the pier at Tanjungpinang. Throughout the long voyage, we had been elbow-to-elbow with scores of Indonesians who had, it seemed, almost as much luggage as we did. As the boat's engine slowed to a steady throb, the passengers began to stir. There seemed to be a lot more expectancy in the air than you would expect on what really was nothing more than a ferry. Several hundred yards away in every direction

157

except that of the pier, fifteen-foot-long dugout canoes hovered, one person at the single oar in the stern, another midship just sitting. With a flurry, a police boat swept up to our side, and three heavily armed officers leapt aboard. Must be customs, I thought. I was right and I was wrong.

When the hull of our ship came within a few yards of the pier, a dozen dugouts shot out from beneath the wooden structure. The canoes that had been orbiting us for the past twenty minutes closed in like we had become an electromagnet and they were iron filings. Simultaneously, the Indonesian passengers on board galvanized into action. The piles of packages they had been guarding assiduously since Singapore became missiles aimed, as best they could, at certain dugout canoes. Because of the total confusion, the only way the goods could find the right target was if everyone yelled at the top of their voices. We four from KSTP in Minnesota were rooted to the spot with astonishment, watching the most primitive smuggling operation in the world. The officers that had come aboard earlier added to the confusion by doing their share of screaming, and there was much waving of drawn pistols, but thankfully, no shots were fired. Even as we bumped gently against the pier, the chaos continued, joined by customs officers on shore, one of them getting a few licks in with his pistol across the side of the head of one smuggler who got a little too close. It was over as quickly as it started. We were the only people left on the ship with anything to declare.

The exhausted customs officers barely glanced at our expensive equipment. They had worn themselves out trying to prevent their countrymen from bringing in radios and calculators from Singapore. They had to save their strength. There were still several boats to come in that day, and they knew what was going to happen.

There were automobiles in Tanjungpinang, but even after ten minutes of furious haggling, we were not prepared to pay the exorbitant amount they wanted to take us and our gear to the hotel. Fortunately, there was an alternative. It must have made a strange sight, this convoy of rickshaws, some piled high with suitcases and trunks and some carrying several wild-eyed television people from across the world. But it beat walking even the half-mile from the harbor to the Hotel Tanjungpinang.

Actually, it didn't look too bad from the outside, and the lobby seemed a trifle cooler than the oppressive heat and humidity of the crowded street, probably because it had no doors and the floor was tiled. So were the walls, rather like a public rest room. But the true charm of the Hotel Tanjungpinang was in its rooms.

I stepped into number 18, hot, dusty, and tired. All I wanted was a refreshing shower and some rest and I would be as good as new. Dropping my bag on the low-lying bed, I noticed the holes in the single grey blanket that barely reached from the foot to the biscuitlike pillow. No matter. Tired as I was, sleeping, even on that uninviting couch, would not be a problem. Nor would the thundering racket that came from the ancient air conditioner. Now, where's the shower? I hadn't noticed at first, but a corrugated steel door swung crazily on one hinge on the left of the room as I walked in. I gingerly pushed it back, and even with one hinge, it had the gall to scream at me. It couldn't help it, rust coated everything that wasn't covered in a green slime of algae and mildew. Now, where's the shower? There wasn't one. There was a sink, but no faucet pointed its nose into it. The tap was on the wall over a huge plastic urn that was half full of tepid water that looked as though the last guest had washed his feet in it. Closer inspection revealed there were other residents in the room. The urn water was actually teeming with life, tiny creatures that wriggled and swam, living their lives unaware that their destiny was to be dashed over my head in a cascade followed by a fast ride to the drain. Other nonpaying guests skittered across the walls and ceiling, tiny lizards, who at least earned their keep by preying on the infinite variety of bugs that filled the air with a steady hum. Hanging on the edges of the urn by a piece of twisted wire was a small saucepan. This was the shower.

My first mistake was emptying the gross water out of the urn. It wasn't hard to do. There was a drain in the center of this closet that passed for a bathroom. All I did was upend the urn, and its rotten contents just flowed away with a satisfying gurgle. My error was not checking to see if the water was running to refill it.

The water in the Hotel Tanjungpinang was turned on for two hours each day, maybe. "Which two hours?" I asked naively. "Hard to say," was the reply. Borrowing a saucepan full of water from Phil, who hadn't squandered his supply of today's ration, I thought I could at least shave. This was to be my second mistake. Naturally, there was no stopper for the sink, but experienced traveler that I am, I knew a handkerchief balled up and jammed in the hole would hold the water in just long enough for a very fast shave. It worked! Somewhat refreshed, I dried my smooth face with the two-foot-square, threadbare cloth I had found folded neatly on the foot of the bed. Feeling victorious, I pulled out my handkerchief and watched the sudsy water drop from sight through the drain . . . right onto my feet. Yes, there was no plumbing. Indeed, there was also no toilet seat *or* toilet paper.

Bright and early the next morning, before the oppressive heat and humidity came down like a blanket on Tanjungpinang, Roger and I paid a visit to the American refugee authorities in their little office, which was no more than a lock-up shop on the main street through town. They told us they would expedite their part of the immigration and health procedures for the Ly family as soon as we could arrange for

160

the Indonesian authorities to release them into our care. Easier said than done.

The only man who could tell us exactly where the Lys were being held and agree to their release was a certain admiral named Wibisono! Praying he hadn't heard we had been using his name constantly to get this far, we called the military camp near town and made an appointment to see the man himself.

Roger and I sat impatiently in a cool anteroom outside the admiral's office. We had been there two and a half hours already, and although there was a lot of coming and going, it was if we were invisible. Watching the impassive faces of the men and women officers as they came and went, doing their duty, whatever it was, I was reminded of what the Indonesian forces were capable of. Eight years earlier, I was working as a reporter for GTV Channel Nine in Melbourne, Australia. I was assigned to go to Timor, which had just been vacated by the Dutch and was in danger of being invaded by the Indonesians. As it happened, my wife was about to present us with our second child, so with a great deal of disappointment, I asked the news director to send another reporter. A week later, the reporter and cameraman from Channel Nine and three staffers, friends of mine, from Channel Seven in Melbourne were lined up against a wall in a little village in Timor and shot to death by the invading Indonesian forces.

I was uncomfortable in the military camp in Indonesia, and it didn't help that they kept us waiting for the entire day. We never got to see Wibisono, but we did get to see his deputy, who, strangely, refused to discuss our plea in the office but insisted we meet him at his home later in the evening.

Whatever we had done, it worked. We were told the Lys were in a camp close to Tanjungpinang and we could watch the American authorities process their immigration request the next day. If that went according to plan and they passed the health requirements, we could take them back to Minnesota, and it would be just in time for Thanksgiving. To celebrate, the four of us decided to go out and eat at the only restaurant in town, a Chinese place just across the street from the Hotel Tanjungpinang. This is not where the locals ate. Their restaurant was, by day, the main road running through town. At five every evening, the traffic stopped flowing and little stalls sprouted like mushrooms all over the pavement. Within minutes, spicy smells began to drift through the streets, beckoning the hungry to eat. It was a colorful and exotic sight, but we wanted to sit down and have someone serve us the best food our money could buy. After all, this was our celebration dinner.

The Chinese restaurant was, like most other businesses in this tropical town, a lock-up shop front. A metal shutter rose every morning, and you simply stepped off the street into the darkness of the building and sat at one of the half-dozen tables. Gary, Phil, Roger, and I selected a table that looked as though it might survive the meal, sat down, and waited to be served. It took a while, because although the cook was visible sweating over an antique stove in the back of the store, the waiter hadn't arrived to work yet. Stirring by the other hopeful diners heralded the arrival of the waiter, a young man with a pencil-thin mustache wearing black stove-pipe pants, a T-shirt with the legend "Death" emblazoned across the chest, and a safety helmet. The safety helmet made sense. With a deafening roar and a cloud of noxious, oily smoke, our waiter rode his filthy motorcycle right off the street into the restaurant, where he casually parked it next to some poor soul's table.

We were not easily deterred from our plan to have the best meal that Tanjungpinang had to offer. We ordered several dishes, not necessarily Chinese since the menu offered the exotic range of Asian food we were becoming accustomed to. As we neared the end of the meal, I noticed two things: The

162

waiter hovered a little too closely and nervously to our table for comfort, and several mangy cats were prowling cautiously along the line of dirt that marked where the door hit the street each night, separating the in from the out.

Inadvertently, we gave the signal. Almost as one, we sat back from our plates and, although there was still lots of food on the table, declared ourselves filled. It was difficult to see who got to the table top first, the waiter, trying to gather up the debris of our meal, or the four scruffy felines that with one leap made it from the street to the free feed they were obviously skilled at stealing each night. Glasses and plates crashed and skittered across the tiled floor. In his efforts to beat the cats to the scraps, the waiter swept as much as he could as quickly as he could into a plastic bowl he carried under one arm. Although we didn't speak Indonesian, Malay, or Chinese, we were sure he was using some very foul language as he fought this nightly battle of the bowl.

Tangjungungat was the name of the camp where thirty-seven-year-old Ly Van Ly, his wife, Kim Dinh Ly, who was thirty-three, and their two children, ten-year-old son Tuan Anh and five-year-old daughter Yen Hai had been for four months. We found them smiling. It was as though their faces were permanently fixed in a happy grin that said without words how happy they were to be so select among so many that they, and they alone, would be leaving soon for the United States. But their joyful countenances belied the misery of their surroundings. Their home was the equivalent of a four-by-eight sheet of plywood—thirty-two square feet of space in a jam-packed wood drying shed. There were many of these sheds, long, low buildings parallel to each other, providing, at least, a roof and four walls to protect their inhabitants from the monsoon rains that poured down each day from the constantly leaden skies. In one corner of their little patch, a small pile of belongings included a battered wok, four

163

bowls, a couple of spoons, an empty can, a small bag of rice, and a jar of preserved fish. It was all they owned, apart from a writing pad and a ball-point pen they constantly used to write to anyone in the world they thought could help them.

The Lys were thin but apparently healthy. We watched them eat their single meal for the day, a little fish and rice. Yen watched our every move with her large, round, dark eyes. A loving child, she attached herself to anyone of us that came close. Her little hand found Gary's big paw, and his eyes filled with tears as he tried to detach himself to operate his camera without hurting the little girl's feelings.

As we filmed this pitiful scene, I glanced around the shed, which teemed with humanity. Vietnamese refugees by the thousands thronged the living spaces and the narrow passage-ways that ran the length of the shed on both sides. An old woman skillfully rolled a cigarette using course local tabacco and ungummed paper. It ended up looking more like a ice-cream cone than a cigarette, but she happily lit it with a match and her face disappeared in wreaths of smoke. A child of about six sat on the dirt floor with one arm in the air as she rocked a baby that snoozed contentedly in a makeshift hammock made from scraps of string and rope that had been scavenged from a variety of sources. Five men and a boy sat on their haunches playing a game with round ivory pieces with black centers that looked somewhat like checkers. Time passed slowly for these people. Many of them had no idea where they would end up, but they were all happy to be here rather than in Vietnam.

Outside the sheds, a large group of young boys played a spirited game of soccer with a green ball. The ankle-deep mud they raced around in hardly slowed them down, and the puddles only served to wash the accumulated mud off the ball. A mother washed a pretty girl by dumping a can full of water over her as she squatted, naked, on the side of the muddy street. At some point, a barbed wire fence had surrounded the sheds. Now broken down and in many places nonexistent, the wire served as a laundry line for the scrubbed-thin clothing the refugees found some way to wash.

Outside one shed, a woman who was unusually large of hip and bosom for a Vietnamese sat behind a tray full of cigarettes, candy, a few dried peppers, and some cans of fish. It was the store, such as it was, and a place to get a few luxuries if you had the money to buy them. Ly Van Ly was one of the more fortunate. He was able to keep his family better fed because he was working as a painter for the camp authorities.

A picnic table covered with an appropriate red, white, and blue striped cloth served as an outdoor office for United States Immigration and Naturalization Service officer Ralph Forster. The four members of the Ly family stood on one side with their right hands raised, palms facing Forster and interpreter Nga Jones, both who stood on the other side. "Do you solemnly swear to tell the truth, the whole truth, and nothing but the truth?" Forster said the words in English, but there was no need for Nga Jones to translate. The four members of the Ly family all nodded enthusiastically, especially little Yen, whose bangs flipped up and down like a shutter as her head snapped her pledge to tell the truth. "Have a seat," said Forster.

It was unusual for the time of the year, but the sun broke through the overcast and lit the little group gathered around the brightly colored table. Within an imaginary semicircle on the mud about twenty-five feet behind the Ly family, there was a kind of no-mans land. But beyond that, it seemed the entire population of the camp had gathered to watch. They stood quietly and passively, their eyes filled with envy. What luck for the Ly family: four men from America, television cameras, and the INS, surely a ticket out of this miserable place.

165

No sooner was the official government interview over than another began. Virgil Westland, a silver-haired, kindly-looking man with wire-rimmed glasses, wearing a smart and surprisingly crisp dark blue shirt, represented a refugee assistance organization called the Joint Volunteer Agency. Westland was explaining the basis and purpose of the interview to the Lys. "First of all, I want to congratulate you on being accepted for resettlement in the United States. I hope you will enjoy your life there." As Nga Jones translated these few simple words, the Lys' permanent smiles became radiant. The two children looked at their parents, and the joy was absolute.

It was four days before Thanksgiving, just enough time to spring this happy group out of the camp and on to the leap-frog journey across the South China Sea and the Pacific Ocean to America. All that remained was the formality of the health check, which was scheduled for the next morning. We were given permission to pick the family up at the camp to take them to the clinic downtown for their examination.

It was a happy group of people that piled haphazardly into a couple of cabs the next morning shortly after dawn. The short drive into town was the first trip outside the camp for the Lys, and they were excited at this positive indication of their imminent freedom. While the children were being examined by the doctor at the clinic, I took advantage of Nga Jones's presence to interview Ly and Kim about their escape from Vietnam. "They tried to get away once before," Nga translated the rapid, and to me undecipherable, Vietnamese that seemed to pour out of the two adults. "But a Vietnamese gang caught them and demanded they give them everything or they would report them to the authorities." "Everything?" I questioned Nga. She asked Ly and Kim again the details of this dreadful night so many months ago as they stood on the edge of freedom. "Yes, everything. Their possessions, their money, even the clothes on their backs." The tragic story continued. On their second attempt, after paying the equivalent of five thousand dollars to a fishing boat captain, the four members of the Ly family left their country. There were thirteen families on the tiny, leaking craft that pitched and tossed in the choppy seas. After a miserable night at sea, they were approached by a Thai fishing boat. This was a terrifying moment, as the refugees knew well. Pirates ranged these dangerous waters, preying on the helpless families, stealing what they had, raping at will, and sometimes murdering their victims.

The fishermen gave them food and water that would last them three days, and they continued puttering south looking for sanctuary. Several days went by, and as their supplies dwindled, they were forced to make a course for the only thing on the horizon, which was an oil rig. It was their only hope. They were welcomed at the German-Malaysian rig and invited to eat on the supply ship that was moored alongside. They were told a Malayan boat would come soon to take them to the mainland, which lay just over the horizon, about forty miles to the west. Three days later, a boat came. They were provided with food and water, and their little battered craft was taken in tow. For whatever reason, the story that they were being taken to Malaya was a lie. Half a day from the oil rig, a crew member of the Malayan patrol boat stepped onto the afterdeck, swung an axe, and cut the tow rope. Once again, the boat load of refugees was at the mercy of the waves and whomever might come across them in these blood-stained waters. They were among the lucky ones spotted by an Indonesian navy ship and towed to relative safety at an island close to Malaya but owned by Indonesia. They had escaped from Vietnam, but there were virtual prisoners in the camps until we showed up.

"Who is next, please?" The white-coated doctor beckoned

to the family, and we gathered our equipment to record the physical examination of Ly and Kim. We were not prepared for the brusqueness of the doctor and the lack of privacy accorded the refugees. "Strip, please. You can keep your underwear on." The doctor's order, given in Vietnamese, was meaningless to us, but averting her eyes and without the courage or confidence to request that the camera be turned off, Kim Ly took off her blouse and pants. She stood stoically as the doctor examined her, and I was struck by her poise as she stood in the center of the crowded room, unaware as she was that out of common decency, Gary had shut off the videocamera. What touched us all was that this proud woman, in her determination to let nothing stand in her way to freedom in America, stood in her pale-blue underwear that were clean but full of holes and gritted her teeth at this indignity.

The tests showed that the Ly family was, by and large, a healthy one, but Kim's X rays showed lesions on her lungs that indicated a previous bout of tuberculosis. This was an unexpected and fateful discovery. With only three days remaining to get the family back to Minnesota in time for Thanksgiving, the medical authorities said a letter must be signed by a doctor in Minnesota who would assume responsibility for follow-up treatment for Kim before their exit papers could be signed. We now were forced to do something we had been avoiding ever since we had arrived in Tanjungpinang, something we dreaded like the plague, something we hoped to avoid at all costs, our worst nightmare. We had to make a phone call!

"Allo, Jakarta. "Allo, Jakarta. Allo, Jakarta." The telephone operator screamed at the top of his lungs with a piercing voice that needed no wires to carry it for miles. The Tanjungpinang telephone office was a tiny shack with its own foul-smelling, oppressive atmosphere on the outskirts of town. It was the only place from which we could place the call to assignment editor Tom Wayne at our office in St. Paul, Minnesota. "Allo, Jakarta. Allo, Jakarta." What hope was there, I wondered, of us making a call halfway around the world if this little man with the big voice in the telephone office in Tanjungpinang couldn't even reach the capitol city of his country? It seemed random, the way he plugged and unplugged the worn cords in and out of the hundreds of holes on his antique telephone switchboard. It had been over four hours. We were hungry, hot, and tired, but we had to stay. As unlikely as it seemed, this was our only chance to get the whole family back in time.

We were startled by the sheer volume of the bell that suddenly started clamoring above a wooden telephone kiosk in a corner of the dark, dusty room. Our call to United States was on the line. I grabbed the phone and said, "Tom?" A tinny, faraway voice replied, "Jason?" The conversation never proceeded beyond that point. Somewhere along the line, among the dozens of operators around the world listening with their hands ready on the plug eager to pull it, one of them did. After more than four hours waiting for the call, we had been cut off—just like that. We were dismayed but relentless. The call had to be made, and we were going to make it. It was evening before the connection was made again, and I hollered at Tom Wayne the instructions for the all-important form. He assured me he would take care of it, and sure enough the document was quickly approved by the appropriate health authorities in Singapore. The Lys were free to leave Indonesia with their continued health care guaranteed under the signature of an unknown doctor in Minnesota named Tom Wayne.

It wasn't a big job to move the Ly family out of their temporary home. The little band of people came out of the dark shed wearing their best clothes. Little Yen looked pretty and bright-eyed in a sea-green cotton top and pants. Her brother Tuan had the same yellow and white knit shirt on that he had worn for the interviews, and his black pants were a little short

169

but adequate. Ly and Kim also wore light clothing, a blue blouse and loose pants for Kim and a white shirt and light jeans for Ly. While they were not barefoot, they wore the only footwear they owned—rubber thongs. They carried everything they possessed in two airline bags they would have no difficulty stowing under the airplane seat. They didn't have much in the way of material possessions, but they were the four happiest people in the world that day.

In one hand, Roger held a piece of paper. It was the official pass releasing the Ly family from the care of the Indonesian authorities. In his other hand, the tiny, trusting fingers of little Yen kept a constant pressure, afraid he might let go and she would have to stay. The little procession passed quietly through the lines of refugees whose time had not yet come. The eyes of the crowd showed a confusion of thought, glad to see this lucky family begin their journey to a new life, sad to think they had to stay and wait.

It took about a half an hour for the 1950 Ford taxi to reach the airport outside Tanjungpinang. It was raining, and the mass of people waiting for the Jakarta flight was jammed into the tiny terminal building. It was hot and noisy, and the Ly family kept looking over their shoulders. They were aware their papers were not entirely in order. A crucial travel document had not yet arrived from the United States. However, they were free to travel within Indonesia and free to try to get a seat on the old twin-engine airliner that swept down from the muggy skies for a bumpy, splashy landing. We and the four family members had tickets, but as is usual on these small airline routes, it was open seating. At least our group didn't have to wrestle with too much baggage. Everybody else did.

It was a shoving match. As it turned out, there were many more passengers than seats, more people and their baggage, which included crates of live chickens, sheaves of bamboo poles, and many odd-shaped, and some evil-smelling, packages. One woman with a distinctive, pockmarked face hefted a large, poorly wrapped parcel that dripped blood for the entire two-hour flight to Jakarta. It was the first flight in their lives for the Ly family and the only flight I have ever taken where people stood in the aisles because they didn't have a seat. Our party, having boarded first as the result of Roger greasing someone's palm at the gate, had seats. Little seats, barely wide enough for a child, the kind of seats where you must keep your elbows tucked in like chicken wings to avoid too familiar contact with your neighbor. There were no tray tables to "make sure they are in an upright position for landing," but they did serve lunch. A flustered flight attendant pushed and shoved her way through the standing-room-only passengers, thrusting small green packages and plastic cups at everyone. The green packages turned out to be squares of gooey rice wrapped in some kind of leaf. The cups were about half full of a sweet, tasteless liquid she said was lemonade.

Three days to go before Thanksgiving. If everything went according to plan, the Ly family had plenty of time to get a plane in Jakarta to Bangkok, where they would take a Northwest Airlines flight to Seattle and then a direct flight to Minneapolis. They would arrive late in the afternoon of November 22.

The first delay came in Jakarta, where the whole party went to the airport only to find the reservations were for the next day. The plane to Bangkok was full, so they would have to come back the next day. Even with that, it was still possible to make Minneapolis by Thanksgiving, a deadline that the Ly family was unaware of but which was important to us.

The breather at least gave us a chance to buy the four refugees a decent meal. We took them to the restaurant at our hotel, a snazzy place with expensive furnishings and food prices to match. The menu was one of the huge, leather-bound affairs written in copperplate and featuring escargot and

171

shrimp cocktails, prime rib and roast duck, oysters and caviar. The four hungry people who had, less than twelve hours before, existed on a handful of fish and rice stared politely at the book that was handed to them by a waiter who was having difficulty disguising his contempt. They couldn't read the English and fancy French names, so Roger simplified for them. He droned down the list, translating as best he could until he mentioned chicken. Chicken. Their eyes lit up. Chicken all around.

Apart from an eight-hour delay in Tokyo and a missed connection in Hong Kong, where there was another opportunity to eat out (chicken), the flights to the United States were comfortable and uneventful. It was raining in the clouds above Seattle, and as the Northwest Airlines 747 lost altitude, the precipitation turned to snow. The Lys stared out of the oval windows at range after range of mountains that seemed to be trying to drive the city into the sea. They had never seen mountains before, and the sight of these white-coated giants veiled in the milky, snow-filled skies filled their faces with wonder. The huge jumbo jet crunched onto the icy runway and taxied slowly to the gate. They had crossed the international date line. It was still Thanksgiving.

The flight to Minneapolis, with only one stop in Spokane, carried only a handful of passengers. Families all over the country were sitting at table together celebrating and giving thanks for the abundance the land and their own hard work provided. The scheduled arrival time of the flight was nine-thirty in the evening, perfect for the event to be broadcast live on the ten o'clock news. In the Twin Cities, mobile microwave trucks were dispatched to the airport. Reporters and photographers, not only from KSTP but from newspapers and radio stations, readied themselves to cover the Ly family reunion. In Afton, Minnesota, the two sons Vu and Liem could hardly contain their excitement, and their aunt looked forward to seeing her sister again after five long years.

After stopping briefly in Spokane, the handful of passengers buckled themselves into their seats for the flight to Minneapolis–St. Paul. Those who glanced out of the window watched a group of maintenance workers spraying de-icing liquid onto the wings of the DC-9. There was some delay before the door was closed and the plane was readied to taxi out, but they were on their way on the last leg of this momentous journey.

Suddenly and inexplicably, the door was reopened, and the flight attendants, pilots, and navigator gathered up their little soft-sided suitcases and garment bags and walked off the airplane. A gate agent announced the bad news: An accumulation of delays on this and other aircraft meant that the crew for this flight would have exceeded their allowable flying hours if they had continued. It was four in the afternoon. The next flight from Spokane to the Twin Cities would not leave until tomorrow, the day after Thanksgiving.

A disappointed but resigned group of weary travelers that included four Vietnamese refugees on the precipice of a new life headed for the Holiday Inn. They had dinner together that night in the hotel restaurant (turkey).

On the flight from Spokane to Minneapolis–St. Paul the next day, Ly Van Ly was asked what he would say to the two sons he hadn't seen since he pushed them on that last ship out of his war-torn country five years before. His voice choking with emotion, this slender man who had been through so much searched for the few English words he knew that would answer the question. "I will say," he faltered and swallowed a lump in his throat. "I will say I love you, more than any people." A single tear slowly rolled down his sallow cheek, and he turned away from the camera and looked out of the window at the blue sky of freedom.

There were cameras at the gate in Minneapolis–St. Paul, and there were cameras following the Ly family as they walked the length of the airbridge toward the terminal. The four of them walked uncertainly toward the lights they could see ahead, then suddenly they glimpsed the two boys. "Liem," Ly shouted, and as a group they broke into a run, leaving behind five-year-old Yen, whose little legs couldn't keep up. They all met, still within the confining walls of the airbridge, a tangle of people hugging, kissing, laughing, and crying. Ly Van Ly picked up his seven-year-old son Vu as if he were a feather. They were together again, and no matter what the calender said, it was time for Thanksgiving.

That was November 23, 1979. Ly Van Ly and his wife, Kim, have been popular employees of Hubbard Broadcasting ever since. Ly is in charge of the stock room, and Kim controls the mailroom. The children are all grown up now and doing well in school. The family owns its own house in Lauderdale, Minnesota, and they share a car.

They are not rich with money by American standards, but they are healthy, happy, and above all, free.

RAINBOW LOVE

OVER THE YEARS, my work has taken me into hospitals all over the world. Whether the healing places have been in the slums of Bogota, Colombia, or in Rochester, Minnesota, they have, universally, been depressing places.

Take, for a good example, St. Lukes in Fargo, North Dakota. St. Lukes is a beautiful, modern, twentieth-century hospital. It is well-run by people who are dedicated to making well again the sick and injured that come through its doors. But simply because it is a hospital, St. Lukes is a grey place.

We came to St. Lukes this spring morning to meet two characters that make this particular hospital special. They both give themselves completely to making this fearful place more friendly, less scary, happier.

The two people we came to meet are well known to all the staff and most of the patients at St. Lukes. But they have never been seen together or at the same time.

We begin our television story by introducing a nun. A

modern nun to be sure but a woman of the cloth nevertheless. Sister Juliana Wisnewski is a striking forty-eight-year-old woman who looks ten years younger than her age and carries with her a degree of elegance and charm rarely found among secular woman let alone nuns.

St. Lukes is a Catholic hospital, and Sister Juliana is its chaplain. We watch as she comforts Gilbert, a brawny man of about sixty who is terminally ill with lung cancer. As Sister Juliana holds his big paw in her long, slender hands, Gilbert says, "It's magnificent. You meet somebody for such a short time and enjoy her so much."

Sister Juliana is a constant, cheerful, and supportive presence in this drab world of needles and operating theaters. The other person we have come to meet is totally different.

Around a corner and into our vision sweeps the most colorful character we've ever seen. The straw boater, baggy pants, smock, and sneakers are fundamentally white but almost totally covered with rainbows. The bright red smile is inches deep and a mile wide. The mop of black, curly hair seems to have a life of its own as this apparition skips by, leaving an invisible but tangible wake of happiness. Not only are rainbows sewn on every part of the clothing and shoes but this picturesque pixie has bright red hearts painted on his or her cheeks.

This, we are told, is "Rainbow Love," a twice-a-month visitor who just sort of appears, spreads around a lot of hugs, gifts, and love and then disappears.

Rainbow Love is weighed down with armfuls of multicolored teddy bears, balloons, and two large shopping bags. Naturally, the bags are covered with every color in the spectrum.

Sister Juliana Wisnewski and Rainbow Love, two identities that in their separate ways bring a ray of sunshine into this shadowy place. Each of them a story unto themselves, but at

176

the same time it's impossible to divide them, because they are one and the same.

"What I'm trying to convey is, it might be real tough, I mean this just might be the pits. But there is hope, and there is a better day. There will be a resurrection. Good Fridays lead to Easter Sundays."

In her dark blue dress and wide silver belt with a large cross for a buckle, Sister Juliana talks to us in the tiny refuge that is the hospital chapel. She often comes here to pray, she says, for the dreadfully sick people she sees every day. It's where she recharges her batteries. A place that gives her strength to watch over the patients as the hospital chaplain and to cheer them up as Rainbow Love.

But it's time for us to meet Rainbow Love once more, to watch the tide of smiles that radiates out from her presence as we travel along the corridors and passageways that connect all the divisions of this large metropolitan hospital.

Suddenly, we are aware of music. It seems to follow us wherever we go. It's a plaintive melody that we all know, a song sung by a frog named Kermit called "The Rainbow Connection," and it is coming from the depths of one of the gaily colored cloth bags swinging from Rainbow Love's arm.

"Why are there so many songs about rainbows and what's on the other side?" sings Kermit, as Rainbow Love hugs a surprised but obviously pleased elderly man she happens to run into on the way to anywhere.

As we watch the antics of the character she created, we hear the words of Sister Juliana explain why Rainbow Love was born. "Though I appear in color and I appear as a rainbow, underneath all of this is the fact that a rainbow is there because some kind of thunderstorm has preceded it."

We are in pediatrics, and this is where Rainbow Love shines. Two little girls about four years old are sharing a crib. Their eyes are like saucers as they gaze in wonder at this smiling clown who doesn't speak but mimes a language they can't fail to understand.

"There is a connection for me, and I might say that sometimes only because of pain do we grow." The words of Sister Juliana Wisnewski. Not content with giving her life to helping others as herself, she creates another person to do double duty.

As we listen to Kermit crooning at the bottom of the bag, "Someday you'll find it. The Rainbow Connection. The lovers, the dreamers, and me. La, da, de, la, leeeee," we watch a three-year-old girl with grey, round eyes and a bandage on her cheek blow a big kiss to her new friend Rainbow Love, who, kneeling in the doorway, throws a kiss back and makes a gigantic heart sign with her arms.

Everyone smiles.

PESKY PANTS FOR
CHRISTMAS

IT WAS SHORTLY after Christmas 1980, and most of the holiday stories had disappeared from the newspapers. But my eyes were drawn to a story tucked away on page six of an out-of-town newspaper that told the incredible tale of Roy Collette, his brother-in-law Larry Kunkel, and a pair of moleskin trousers that I would dub and would forevermore be called the "pesky pants."

The story told of how Larry had received, as a Christmas gift from his mother, a pair of moleskin pants. That was in 1964, and Larry wore them just long enough to realize they were a lousy garment. In the frigid winters of his hometown of Owatonna in southeastern Minnesota, the pants froze so stiff he had difficulty walking. So come Christmas 1965, Larry bestowed the pants on his unsuspecting brother-in-law Roy. A couple of cold days later, Roy realized why his brother-in-law had been so unusually generous, and, you've guessed it, back they went to Larry as a gift on December 25, 1976. So

179

it began. The two relatives by marriage passed the pants back and forth every Christmas for years, until one day Roy was puzzled by the absence of a familiar package under his tree. But there was a long tube, with a diameter of only an inch or so, marked "To Roy from Larry." It couldn't be the pants, thought Roy, there is no way they could be rammed into such a thin tube. Roy was wrong. It was the birth of a traditional contest between the two men to present the pants in packaging that at first was just meant to confuse but by the time we caught up with them had reached a grand scale that was about to make them both famous throughout the world.

Just before Christmas 1981, I called Roy and told him I would like to come and record the delivery of the pants when they arrived that year from Larry, who at that time was living in Illinois. "They're already here," said Roy. "Come down any time you want."

When we pulled up outside Roy's house on the outskirts of Owatonna, he was outside waiting for us. In his hand, he had a Christmas card, which he read aloud as the camera rolled. "Merry Christmas, Roy. The pants are in the glove compartment of the car. Fondest regards, Larry." The car, a 1971 Ford Gremlin, was sitting in the middle of Roy's driveway. It had been crushed into a three-foot-square cube!

Roy told us later it had taken many days of hard work, using diamond saws, oxyacetylene torches, chisels, and even a jackhammer, to extricate the pesky pants. He said he even considered using dynamite! But get them out he did. They were undamaged because Larry had taken care to enclose them in a steel tube.

By now, the game had taken on two simple rules. The brothers-in-law had agreed that no money should be spent by either in packaging or delivering the pants. And it should not be impossible to unpack them. The first rule didn't inhibit the two men as it might many others. They both worked in in-

180

dustry and had many friends who would willingly donate time and material and even transportation to be part of what had become a traditional part of Christmas for everyone that knew them. And now, with our involvement, people all over the world were also enjoying the joke.

Even as Roy and his sons sought the pants in the tangle of steel and chrome that had once been a car, his fertile mind was working on how to get his own back, or give Larry his own back, whichever you prefer.

On Christmas Eve 1982, we watched as the pants were loaded onto a truck for their journey back to Larry. The tractor tire was seven feet across. It still had a huge steel hub in the center, and, Roy told us with evident glee, "The sides of the tire are three inches thick." A replaced rubber circle showed where the pants had been introduced into the huge wheel, along with six thousand pounds of concrete. The raised lettering on the side had an addition in white paint. It now read:

"And," Roy chortled, "the pants are in a plastic tube so he can't track them down with a metal detector." These guys were getting sophisticated.

181

Larry, who was still living in Illinois, later told us that he couldn't find a tool that could penetrate the rubber tire without a great deal of backbreaking labor. Luckily, the concrete inside hadn't completely set up, so he was able to retrieve the pants in just a few days, although he made a horrible mess.

In 1983, Larry moved back to his hometown of Owatonna, which meant we were able to follow the adventures of what by now were a very battered pair of pesky pants as they passed back and forth between the two men, who once again were living in the same town.

Larry's penchant for secrecy meant we had no idea what to expect as we set up our camera outside an industrial building in Owatonna just before Christmas. The huge doors swung open at a signal from Larry, and the biggest forklift I had ever seen shuddered into action beneath its top-heavy load. It was a rocket ship that would never leave the ground, sixteen feet high and constructed of four-inch steel tubes full, of course, of concrete. We followed its ponderous journey through the town and out to the suburbs where a nervous Roy paced back and forth on his driveway. Roy was nervous because his brother-in-law had been kind enough to warn him to get all his cars out of his garage if he had any intention of using them in the immediate future.

The word had got around, and there was quite a crowd of friends, family, and the just plain curious waiting outside Roy's house. The forklift gently deposited its six-ton load on the blacktop. "My, my," was all Roy could say, struck almost dumb by the sheer generosity of his brother by marriage. "My, my," he said as the forklift driver kindly lifted him up to get a close look at his gift. He came down to the ground twice, once when the tongues of the machine dropped him off and again when Larry told him the pants were in a plastic tube somewhere in the hundreds of feet of concrete-filled pipes.

182

"But," Larry said grinning from ear to ear, "there are fourteen dummy tubes in there too."

By 1984, the two jokers had been sending the pants back and forth for almost twenty years. It was not an anniversary that Roy wanted to celebrate. He persuaded Larry to call it a day, and in a moment of trust he would live to regret, he took the pants over to Larry's place of work, where Larry promised to laminate them between two pieces of glass for presentation back to his mother at the end of the year.

Just before Christmas, I had a call from Larry. "If I were you, I'd have your camera outside Roy's house this weekend, Jason," he said. "I'll say no more. See you then." And he hung up.

We knew something was up, but the trusting Roy was expecting Larry to arrive carrying the pants under his arm. "What is this!" cried Roy as a huge truck with its back wheels spinning madly on the icy driveway tried to maneuver the car it was towing up to the front of his house. No wonder the truck was having problems. The car, a 1974 Camaro, was obviously carrying a full load. Larry, of course, reveling in his rotten double cross of his brother-in-law, was just delighted to be able to tell everyone there, especially Roy, what he had done. "Well, when we tried to fill the car with concrete, it started to bulge dangerously at the sides, so we reinforced them with bulletproof glass." Roy's pensive response was, "You'll be sorry next year." And you know, he was right.

Nineteen eighty-five is memorable because it was the year that everyone struggled to resolve a puzzle called Rubik's Cube, and Larry got his. Larry's "Rubik's Cube" arrived on a flatbed trailer just before Christmas. It was about six feet square and had a Christmas tree, complete with lights, sitting on top. It took another large forklift to get it off the truck and onto Larry's driveway, where it was obviously going to stay for some time. Roy explained, "The outside is just plain old

183

plywood, but it covers two thousand feet of hardwood one-by-fours laminated together with thousands of hardened steel staples, and that's just the exterior overcoat." Larry stood with his mouth open, astounded by the devotion of his brother-in-law, who was obviously just hitting his stride. "In the center," crowed Roy, "is a two-foot square of concrete, not just any old concrete but a special mix that its makers claim can defy any attempt to smash it apart." Roy paused and stood proudly beside his creation for the photographers, but he couldn't resist a final dig. "I know how you like puzzles, Larry. Merry Christmas."

In later years, Larry always claimed that getting the pants out of that special concrete mix in the "Rubik's Cube" was the worst experience of his life.

"It would appear there is a Ford in my future." Roy stared dejectedly at what was going to keep him busy for a long time in the new year. It was a Ford sure enough. A very old car that was enjoying one last hurrah before it met a long-overdue end at the wreckers. But for now, it was the center of everyone's attention as it rested on Roy's driveway in Owatonna a few days before Christmas 1986. The car was painted in two rather festive shades of red and green, and as Larry threw open the tailgate with a flourish, everyone gasped at his audacity. Lit by a series of Christmas candles were stacks of heavy-looking electric motors and generators. "The bolts on every unit are welded shut, the motors are welded to each other, and they are all welded to the car." Larry stood back so the knot of people gathered around a tired-looking Roy could get a better look at Larry's work of art. "Somewhere in there there's a pair of brown trousers, just for you. Merry Christmas, Roy."

Roy spent weeks trying to figure out where his devious brother-in-law had hidden those pesky pants. Knowing by now that doing anything obvious would probably be a total waste of time, he began by looking in the back panels of the car. Sure enough, there they were. The whole mishmash of at least a hundred and fifty old electric motors was nothing more than a red herring. It was an easy way to end this long-running practical joke. Roy, with the pants in his possession, once again approached Larry with a suggestion that they bring the gag to an end. "Sure," said Larry. "I'm too busy with my new job anyway to spend weeks every year either hiding or looking for those pesky pants. But let's do it in style. We should burn them ceremoniously." "Fine by me," said Roy, and they set a date for the end of the story.

When we arrived at Roy's house, he was in high spirits. "This is it," he told us as soon as we arrived. "Here are the pants, and this is the end." He was serious. A large fire was keeping a lot of people warm outside the house. We had to wait because Larry was late. "Tell you what we've decided to do, Jason." Roy had pulled me off to one side to alert me to a small change of plan. "Larry suggested it would be more spectacular for your camera if we tied the pants between his four-wheel-drive vehicle and mine and pulled them apart before we burned them."

We should have known something about this plan wasn't strictly kosher when Larry showed up with the rope. But who were we to interfere? With a great deal of messing about, Larry took charge of tying the pants equidistant between the two cars, which stood back to back about fifteen feet apart with their engines running. Roy was jubilant. He sat in the driver's seat of his vehicle and positively crowed about how this was indeed the end of a joke that he said had become a nightmare.

Larry had a strange intense look about him as the two cars edged apart and the rope began to tighten. "Okay, let's do it," shouted Roy, and they gunned their engines. Like butter, the rope parted at Roy's end. Larry took off at about fifty miles an hour and immediately disappeared into the winter mist. Roy, too late by far, tried to give chase but ten minutes later came back. He was not amused. He didn't think it at all funny fifteen minutes later when the phone rang and it was Larry. "I'm on my way to St. Louis on business, Roy, but I'll be back in plenty of time to wrap your Christmas present for next year." Despite having been double-crossed twice by his unscrupulous brother-in-law, Roy had regained his sense of humor. "Wouldn't be a pair of pants by any chance, would it, Larry?"

After appearing on the nationally televised show "Incredible Sunday," where Larry and Roy told hosts John Davidson and Christine Ferrare of their exploits, it was no surprise to us that there was a large crowd waiting outside Roy's house just before Christmas 1988 to see how Larry was going to deliver the pesky pants.

The first indication that their arrival was imminent was the deep-throated rumble of a struggling eighteen-wheeler. Then the huge, white tractor trailer turned the corner and revealed its load. It was a space capsule, or at least a very reasonable facsimile of one. Actually, it was the entire business end of a concrete truck standing on its big end. Painted white, it was emblazoned with "United States Command Module Roy '88." It was twelve feet high and eight feet in diameter. That would explain why the next thing to arrive was a huge mobile crane that lumbered up the suburban street like a praying mantis looking for a meal.

It took Larry and six volunteer helpers nearly an hour to unload the space capsule. The problem was its weight. It was filled, he said, with scrap wire rope, tempered glass, and, of course, thousands of pounds of concrete. And Larry said, "Somewhere in there is a very special pair of moleskin pants, just for you, Roy. Merry Christmas."

186

The last shot we got of these two men as we took our leave just before Christmas 1988 was when Roy turned to his brother-in-law and said, "Well, I guess like we've said before, It's not the gift, it's the package."